# HAMPTON AND TEDDINGTON PAST

First published 1995
by Historical Publications Ltd
32 Ellington Street, London N7 8PL
(Tel: 0171-607 1628)

© **Borough of Twickenham Local History Society
and Ken Howe**

**ISBN 0 948667 25 7**
British Library Cataloguing-in-Publication Data
A catalogue record for this book is available from the British Library.

Typeset in Palatino by Historical Publications Ltd
Reproduction by G & J Graphics, London EC1
Printed in Zaragoza, Spain by Edelvives.

## The Illustrations

With the exception of those listed below, the illustrations were supplied by the authors. We are grateful to the following for their kind permission to reproduce pictures from their collections:

Bamber Gascoigne: *26, 95*
London Borough of Richmond upon Thames: *21, 38, 49, 75, 82, 96, 115, 116, 117, 118*
The MCC: *88*
The Royal Parks, Bushy Park Archive: *137*

# HAMPTON AND TEDDINGTON PAST

John Sheaf
Ken Howe

HISTORICAL PUBLICATIONS

# Acknowledgments

The earliest histories of the two areas surveyed in this history were *The History and Topography of Hampton-on-Thames*, by Henry Ripley (1884), and the description of Teddington contained in *The Environs of London*, Vol. III Middlesex by the Rev. Daniel Lysons, published nearly a hundred years earlier in 1795. Subsequent histories and studies of both Hampton and Teddington are listed under Further Reading on pp 140/1, but the authors would like to acknowledge particularly the substantial contributions to the history of Hampton made by the late Gerald Heath, whose writing is a model of accuracy and conciseness. He was extremely generous in the amount of information he supplied, and Joan Heath has been particularly helpful in supplying additional material. We would also like to acknowledge the help and encouragement of many friends in the Borough of Twickenham Local History Society, especially those on the Publications Sub-committee and, of course, those members upon whose work we have drawn. We have also been considerably helped by the publications of the Teddington Society History Research Group.

Acknowledgment is also due to Sharman Sheaf who not only typed much of the original Hampton part of the manuscript, but who showed great forbearance as the project gathered pace.

Many other people have assisted in the production of this book, but the following deserve a special mention: Jane Baxter and Chris Turfitt of Twickenham Reference Library, Sue Osbourne of the National Physical Laboratory Library, Gwen and Bob Tough, Colin Pain, John Ryan, Martin Ellengorn, Margaret Baker and Anthony Cartledge for providing some of the illustrations and Tony Cannings for reproducing many of the pictures used.

We hope that this volume, which in part draws upon the research of others, will whet the appetite of many readers and make them eager to explore the source material noted under Further Reading.

**John Sheaf and Ken Howe**

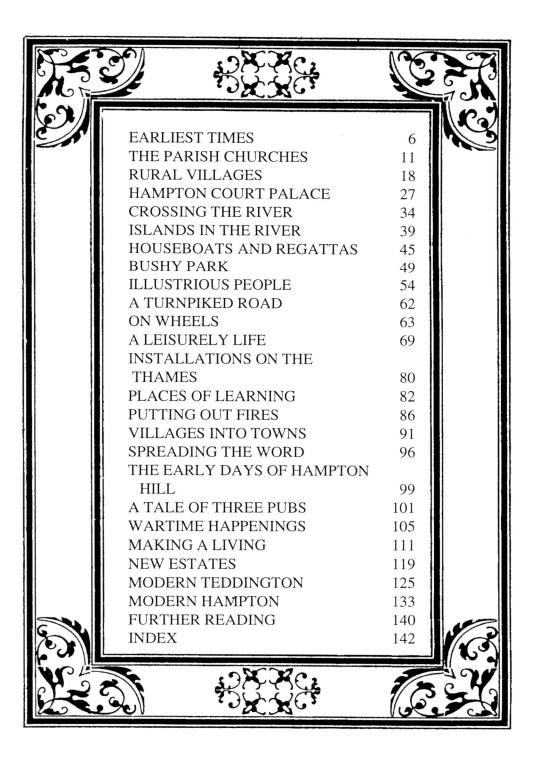

1.  *View of the old St Mary's church, Hampton, with the Bell and the ferry, c.1800.*

# Earliest Times

The earliest prehistoric evidence for the area of Teddington and Hampton has been lost. Bones of ox and reindeer dating from the period that the great ice sheets covering much of England melted – *c*.440,000BC – were found in Lavender's gravel pits at Teddington in the 1930s and came into the possession of Councillor C. Carus-Wilson of Strawberry Hill who exhibited them, along with other parts of his collection, first at Twickenham Public Library and later at the Twickenham Museum at York House. When the Museum closed about 1938, all animal exhibits were to have been transferred to the Natural History Museum, but there is some doubt that they ever reached their destination and they have been missing since that time.

From the Mesolithic period, about 7,000BC when Britain was still joined to the European continent, large quantities of flint and antler tools and weapons have been found at Hampton and Teddington, par-

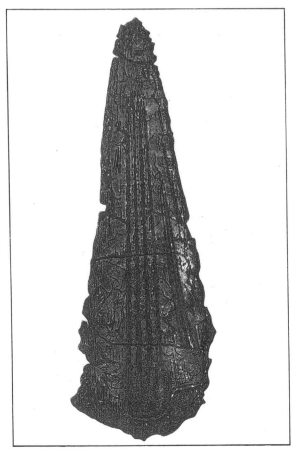

2. *Bronze Age dagger from Teddington Barrow, drawn by Rev. Thomas Hugo.*

*3. Flint axe from Cannon Field.*

ticularly during house development at Cannon Field.

Neolithic man began to settle and farm, and enclosures of land have been excavated at nearby Staines, Runnymede, Heathrow and Shepperton. Once again, stone and bone artefacts were discovered and recently sherds of pottery from this period have been found at Bushy Park.

Teddington's finest monument is the Bronze Age barrow in Sandy Lane, excavated in 1854 by the Surrey Archaeological Society, which appears to have been the burial place for a warrior chief. A fine bronze dagger was found, illustrated here but, like the councillor's bone remains, after exhibition it seems to have disappeared. Further misfortune occurred with a cache of flint celts, found during the building of Clarence Road. These were exhibited by William Niven, architect of St Alban's church, to the Society of Antiquaries, but these too were lost.

Tom Greeves carried out an archaeological survey of Bushy Park in 1993 on behalf of the Department of the Environment. Previously two prehistoric flints had been found there and in the course of the survey, two separate sherds of pottery, one medieval and one from the Bronze Age were found. As word of the survey spread people came forward with finds of their own, many from the roots of trees brought down in the storms. These included two Saxon spindle-whorls and some medieval Surrey whiteware pottery, all indicating an earlier occupation than had been thought.

Evidence of 'ridge and furrow' agriculture from the medieval period and beyond is still visible today in the Park, particularly between the area to the west of the Diana Fountain and up towards the Storeyards.

Greeves summed up the survey by saying: 'It is very unlikely that there is an equivalent area of Middlesex, or indeed, Greater London, where one can see so clearly the overall pattern of a 'classic' medieval open field. Even in their eroded state the survival of several kilometres of medieval furlong baulks, often associated with ridge and furrow, and probably dating back at least 600-700 years is astonishing.'

## THE ROMANS

At the time of the first Roman invasion in 54BC, Middlesex, of which Hampton and Teddington were part, was ruled by the Catuvellanni, a British tribe whose centre of government was at St Albans. Caesar noted their dwellings as 'mean habitations constructed for the most part of reeds and wood.' One of their main pastimes was hunting and they established parks for this purpose – it is possible that Bushy Park dates from this period, though there is no evidence to support this suggestion.

Until recently there was little evidence of Roman occupation in this area. An urn filled with burnt bones, discovered in a house at Hampton Wick, was thought to be Roman, but no full description of it was made and it too has disappeared. Some pottery, possibly Roman, was found in the garden of Oak Cottage in Teddington in the 1950s, but the items were lost before being fully examined.

Montagu Sharpe wrote that in 1808 a 'tothill' stood opposite the gates to Bushy Park, which was removed during the course of road widening. This was thought to be an artificial mound about the size of a haystack, built by the Romans as a survey point and latterly used as a look-out post. It was one of six known to exist in Middlesex. It seems remarkable, however, that a tothill was built so close to the barrow – perhaps these two structures were one and the same.

Edward Jesse, one time H.M. Superintendent at Hampton Court thought, from the evidence of so many Roman weapons dredged from both banks of the Thames at Kingston, that this was the place where the Romans originally crossed the river in their first invasion under Caesar. It is now more widely held that the weapons were likely to have been votive offerings and nothing to do with past battles.

In 1992 excavations in Lower Teddington Road, Hampton Wick, produced an astonishing amount of Roman pottery. More recently a Roman villa has been discovered on the site of St John's Hospital, Twickenham, and traces of a farm have been found by the Chertsey Road.

4. *Excavation in Cannon Field, c1920*

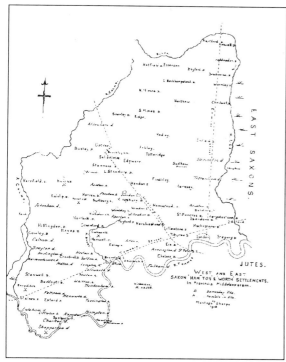

5. *Map of Saxon Middlesex. After the withdrawal of the Romans, the Britons hired mercenary troops of Jutes to defend the shores of the South Coast. However, this proved to be an uneasy alliance and eventually the Jutes fell out with the Britons and drove them out of Kent and Middlesex in AD473. At the same time the East Saxons were establishing footholds in Essex and the West Saxons had gained ground in Hampshire in AD495. They defeated the Jutes at Wimbledon in AD568 and they then controlled all of Middlesex and London until the time of the Danish attacks about AD850. The Saxon settlements of Hampton, Hampton Wick and Teddington were established between these dates.*

## ANGLO-SAXONS

It is from the period of the Anglo-Saxons that the place names Hampton and Teddington derive. It is thought that Hampton comes from *hamm*, meaning a large bend in the river, and *ton*, meaning settlement or farm. The 'wick' of Hampton Wick could denote a dairy farm, but recent research into the prevalence of the word *'wic'* in the Mercian period suggests that it could also mean 'trading place' as in *Lundenwic* (on the Strand), Ipswich, Harwich etc. Hampton Hill is a comparatively new name. The area in 1650 was known as 'The Common' and from *c*.1800 as New Hampton – the name Hampton Hill came into use around 1870. Teddington has the same second element, the first deriving from 'Tuda's people'. The only Tuda mentioned in the *Anglo-Saxon Chronicle* was the Bishop of Lindisfarne, who died during the plague of AD664. It seems unlikely that he should be the same as the Tuda of Teddington, but given the close proximity of Kingston, where six Saxon kings were crowned, it is not out of the question.

## THE MANORS

Both areas were divided into manors at some time before the Norman Conquest of 1066. The manor of Teddington belonged to Benedictine monks located in Staines and it was they, it is thought, who first built a chapel dedicated to St Mary in Teddington. In its turn Staines and its various possessions were granted to the new abbey of St Peter (today's Westminster Abbey) in AD785. A charter – almost certainly forged but probably based on a valid one – of AD971 confirmed the grants of 'the ruined cell of Staines with its appurtenances Tutington, Halgeford [Halliford], Feltham and Eclesford' to St Peter's. Though there is no mention of the manor of Teddington during the reign of Edward the Confessor, or indeed in the Domesday Book of 1086, there seems to be no doubt that it was still a possession of his Westminster abbey, and it remained so until 1536 when it became part of the Hampton Court estate.

Hampton manor at the time of the Domesday Book (1086) was owned by Walter de St Valery, and it remained in his family until 1217. Between 1237 and 1514 it belonged to the Knights Hospitaller: from them Wolsey purchased the lease and there built his palace of Hampton Court. As we shall see, the manor and the building were acquired by Henry VIII in 1529.

Population at the time of the Domesday survey included only 41 villagers and four smallholders for Hampton, Hampton Wick and Teddington, which suggests a total of 200 people. By 1600 this had risen to around 600 and after over 100 deaths from plague in 1603, the number reached about 1150 in 1700 – both these figures referring only to Hampton and Hampton Wick.

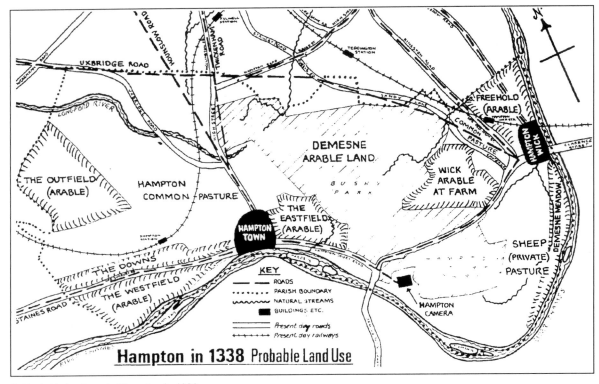

*6. Probable land use in Hampton in 1338.*

## HAMPTON IN THE 14TH CENTURY

Remarkably, we have a good idea of land use in Hampton in 1338. This is because a survey was sent that year by the Prior of the Hospital of St John, who owned the manor, to the Master of the Order, concerning the Order's possessions in England. Exactly 500 years later a copy of this was found by the Rev. Lambert B. Larkins in the Valetta Public Library in Malta while he was on holiday there, and an expanded description was published by the Camden Society in 1857. The information in this was later examined thoroughly in two papers written by Peter Foster for the Borough of Twickenham Local History Society.

The Order of the Knights Hospitaller or of St John of Jerusalem was a military monastic order founded during the eleventh century, ostensibly to protect pilgrims visiting holy places in Palestine, especially when the country was in the control of Islam. To support itself in Palestine, and later in Rhodes and Malta, the Hospitallers set up an international organisation to gather funds and a branch was formed in England in the twelfth century – it later took over the possessions, which included the Temple in Fleet Street, of another Order associated with the Crusades, the

Knights Templar. The Hospitallers bought the manor of Hampton from Henry de St Albans in 1236, although the Hospitallers had owned property in the area for at least fifty years before.

The Hampton manor house was known as a 'camera', that is, a small establishment with land. There were several timber-framed buildings (some with tiled roofs), houses, barns, a chapel and a kitchen, accommodation for visitors and a hall, all probably arranged around a courtyard. These buildings are thought to have stood on the site of Hampton Court Palace.

There were, according to the survey, 800 acres of land, probably rented out for barley and rye, which covered much of the extent of today's Bushy Park (which today has 1099 acres). There were also 40 acres of meadow by the Thames.

In addition there was pasture for 24 oxen, 18 cows, 10 store cattle and 2,000 sheep which, it can be deduced, were of the short-haired variety. Sheep were much smaller then, weighing perhaps 40lbs instead of a modern 200lbs. There was a fish weir in which were set nets or fish traps (this dates back to before 1200), and a pigeon house.

7. *The front of old St Mary's church, Hampton.*

# The Parish Churches

## ST MARY, HAMPTON

Both the parish churches of Hampton and Teddington are dedicated to St Mary. St Mary the Virgin in Hampton has stood on its present site since at least 1342, when we have a record of the first vicar. The date of the earliest building is unknown – it is not mentioned in Domesday Book, but it was probably there by the early thirteenth century, soon after the Knights Hospitaller came to Hampton. They had a preceptory at Hampton by 1180 and the Prior of the Order became lord of the manor in 1239.

The old church was completely demolished in 1829 and we therefore have to rely on paintings, prints and some surviving descriptions and documentary evidence to gain an impression of it. The chancel, built of flint and stone, was probably part of the medieval church, though it had had alterations and additions over the years. The tower was of red brick, but this had been rebuilt in 1679, replacing one of flint and stone which had become unsafe. The north aisle was built in 1726 as well as a vault beneath and a vestry room at the north-west corner.

It has been said that the nave, south aisle and porch replaced the originals 'about the time of Henry VII', but there is no documentary evidence for this. Certainly the main body of the church is described as being of red brick unlike the chancel which was clearly much older.

In addition, there was a large schoolroom on the north side of the chancel at the east end of the north aisle, a 'venerable, barn-like building', which communicated internally with the church.

At the summit of the tower was a lantern-shaped cupola constructed of wood, which housed the quarter-of-an-hour service bell. This cupola was struck by lightning in 1827 and sent crashing to the ground.

A writer in 1797 describes Hampton from Molesey Hurst: 'her brick church in pre-eminence, with fresh painted and accommodating covered benches in the churchyard; whence is an unparalleled command of the river'.

8. *St Mary's Hampton c.1800. The building on the left-hand side of the picture is modern-day No. 1 Thames Street (formerly known as Riverdale). It is a fine Georgian building and dates from 1760-70. It was the home of T. Foster-Knowles, who founded the Cottage Hospital, for over fifty years from 1891. The building on the river foreshore is Ferry House, demolished 1914 and between it and the church is the old Bell inn, burnt down in 1892. To the right of the church is a previous vicarage, built in 1731.*

The interior contained galleries on three sides, with a singing loft for the choir near the roof. At the east end the pulpit was apparently a grand affair, having a 'basement' reserved for the use of the clerk, a second-tier serving as a reading desk, while the 'upper stratum' was for the delivery of sermons.

There were many fine monuments, a number of which have been preserved in the new building, as have some impressive coffins from the old vaults. Monuments from the old church, preserved in the present one, include those to Dame Sibel Penn (nurse to Edward VI), Nicholas Pigeon (benefactor to Hampton School), John Beard (celebrated tenor) and David Garrick (nephew of the actor).

The old church was demolished in 1829 and the present building opened in 1831. The new St Mary's can accommodate approximately twice as many people as its predecessor. It was designed by Edward Lapidge in white brick with stone dressings in gothic revival style, with a square pinnacled tower at the west end. The consecration in 1831 was attended by a royal party including Queen Adelaide.

A number of changes to the church were initiated during the time of the Rev. Prebendary Digby Ram, who was a very popular vicar from 1882-1911 (having

*9. Interior of the rebuilt St Mary's, Hampton.*

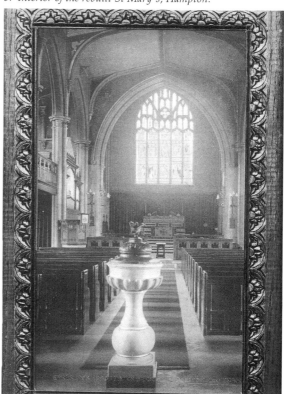

10. *The rebuilt St Mary's church, Hampton in c.1910. In front of the church, by the riverside, is Langshaw's the boatbuilders, advertising launches and boats to let.*

previously served for a very short time in Teddington). New pews were installed in 1884, replacing the old box pews, and in 1887 to mark the Golden Jubilee of Queen Victoria the chancel was added at the east end.

Since that time a number of stained-glass windows have been added by various benefactors. The mural on the west wall was painted in 1952-3 by Rev. Geoffrey M. Fraser, son of the well-known graphic artist, Eric Fraser. Its left-hand panel depicts people from Hampton's local history, and the right-hand panel shows officers of the church and members of the congregation at the time of the painting.

## A PARISH CHURCH RESTORED

Teddington's St Mary's has only in recent years been re-established as the parish church. In the early thirteenth century it was still a chapelry attached to Staines church, but by the end of the Middle Ages it controlled an independent parish.

The church has had some colourful incumbents. Matthew Rendall was suspended by Archbishop Laud in 1634 for preaching a sermon lasting longer than an hour. Thomas Traherne (1637-74), was a poet and mystic; he was vested with the care of Teddington parish (we do not know his official title) almost

certainly because of the patronage of Sir Orlando Bridgeman, an influential local resident, to whom he was already chaplain. He died at Bridgeman House and is buried in Teddington church. Most of his works were to remain unknown until 1896, when William T. Brooke purchased two manuscripts for a few pence from a London bookstall. One contained 37 poems in Traherne's own handwriting and the other was the manuscript of *Centuries of Meditations* – these were subsequently published in 1903 and 1908 respectively; other work by Traherne has been discovered since and as recently as 1967 the manuscript of *Commentaries of Heaven* was rescued from a bonfire.

Dr Stephen Hales was priest from c.1709 to 1761. He was probably the first permanent parish priest in Teddington and there was no vicarage provided when he arrived. The population then was about 450, but even then the church was too small and in a bad state of repair. Hales organised the renovation of the roof and the tower, built a gallery, enlarged the churchyard, and installed a new church bell which was much louder than its predecessor 'to be heard at a much greater distance, not only for the benefit of the serious and well disposed but also as a constant memento to the Careless, the Negligent and the Profane.'

11. *St Mary's church, Teddington. From a print published in 1809.*

12. *Rev. Stephen Hales, parish priest of Teddington for over fifty years. He is recorded as having made six women do public penance during his ministry.*

A new north aisle was added and finally in 1754 the old timber tower was replaced by one in brick. What Hales did not record in the parish register was that he contributed £200 of his own money towards this work, almost half the cost and more than two years' income as incumbent of Teddington. The parish registers do record his habit of imposing penance on female parishioners for misdemeanours. During the period 1723 and 1743 this happened six times, each time as a punishment for fornication or adultery; only once, in 1732, did he inflict this indignity on a man. The woman in each case had to stand outside the church in a white sheet, barefoot during morning service, and was then brought in and preached at and prayed over, before being restored to communion.

Hales, who was a physiologist, inventor and prominent in the formation of the Royal Society of Arts, was also involved in the installation of a system whereby springs on the common were intercepted so that they could drain into a pond which then supplied and flushed the open drain that ran the length of the High Street. Typically, Hales records in the parish register that the outflow of this supply was sufficient to fill a two-quart vessel in '3 swings of a pendulum, beating seconds, which pendulum was 39 + 2/16ths inches long from the suspending nail to the middle of the plumbet or bob.

13. *Rev. John Cosens.*

14. *Rev. Daniel Trinder.*

Hales is regarded as the founder of plant physiology, but he also did some experimental work in animal physiology, specially relating to blood pressure. When he published his best known work, *Haemestatics,* he wrote to a fellow clergyman scientist admitting that he had been responsible for the death of sixty animals and stated that further experiments 'would probably cause the death of 200 or 300 animals, so I do not think it proper for one of our profession to engage any further on it.'

Alexander Pope was one of his friends, although he did not approve of his work on animals and referred to him as 'Plain Parson Hale'. 'I shall be very glad to see Dr Hales, and always love to see him, he is so worthy and good a man. Yes, he is a very good man; only I'm sorry he has his hands so imbrued in blood. What! he cuts up rats? Ay, and dogs too!'

Frederick, Prince of Wales, was a great admirer of Hales' work and frequently made surprise visits to Teddington. After Frederick's death, Hales accepted the post of Clerk of the Closet to the Princess Dowager, although he did not allow this to interfere with his parochial work. Throughout his life he inveighed against the evils of drink and published *A Friendly Admonition to the Drinkers of Brandy and Other Distilled Spirituous Liqueurs* in 1734. Whereas his other parish at Farringdon was 'one of the most orderly parishes in England, I wish I could say the same of Teddington, which being unhappily with the Gin Bills of Mortality, grows continually from bad to worse.'

Hales invited John Wesley to preach at Teddington. Of that first meeting Wesley said 'How well do philosophy and religion agree in a man of sound understanding!'.

John Cosens, his successor and also a poet, was robbed by highwaymen at the gates of Horace Walpole's Twickenham house. The Rev. Daniel Trinder, who became vicar in 1857, brought a return to high-church traditions and divided the parish in the process. He was accused of popery for preaching in a surplice and introducing *Hymns Ancient and Modern*. Feelings became so strong that a section of the congregation broke away and founded Christ Church in Station Road, which allied itself with the Free Church of England. This high-church policy, extended by Trinder's successor in 1884, F. Leith Boyd, was maintained until recent times.

15. *St Alban's church, built to the size of a Gothic cathedral, supplanted St Mary's as parish church for over a hundred years.*

In 1833 the capacity of St Mary's was increased from 413 to 599, paid for by public subscription, including a grant of £50 by the king and queen. But the rising population after the coming of the railway put too much strain on the facilities and Boyd determined on a new and far larger church. William Niven, an architect living at Udney House, designed a new church on the lines (and size) of a French cathedral. Such plans did not meet with the approval of all parishioners. R.D. Blackmore, the writer, who lived locally wrote to a friend that: 'They are building a thumping thing in this parish, which is to cost £30,000 – then to be left unfinished, that is as regards the Tower. I look upon it as a great absurdity and a piece of useless ostentation, for there is not, and will probably not be during the 20th century the population to fill the nave.'

The 'thumping thing' was St Alban's, which was opened in 1889 as the new parish church of Teddington. However, after the Second World War the falling congregation led to it being deregistered. Curiously, the building was not completed until 1993, by which time it was already redundant as a church, and housed instead a centre for the performing arts. Blackmore's prediction had come to pass, and St Mary's became once more the parish church in 1967.

16. *St Mary's church, Teddington.*

17. *John Norden's map of Middlesex, 1610.  One of the earliest maps showing an early spelling as Tuddington and Kingsto Wyke for Hampton Wick.*

# Rural Villages

## HAMPTON

The core of the old village of Hampton is represented in the triangle of roads that is now High Street, Church Street and Thames Street. In addition, three through routes have determined the present road plan of the area – first the Upper Sunbury Road to Staines, second the Lower Sunbury Road to Chertsey, and third the High Street itself which leads to Twickenham. In other places roads have developed from field trackways and boundaries, many of which may still be traced in their modern form.

In the medieval period and much later land was farmed in large open fields. The West field bordered the river on the south, the modern-day Oldfield Road on the north, stretched to the Sunbury border on the west, and back to Hampton town on the east. The Waterworks was to cover much of this area. North of the village lay Warfield, perpetuated today in Warfield Road. The Oldfield referred to in the street name lay north of the West field adjoining what was then Kenton Road – much of its extent is preserved today in the courses of Oldfield Road and Priory Road. The sharp bend where the war memorial cottages are located in Oldfield Road marks the south-eastern corner of the field. To the east of the village lay the Eastfield. This arable land was to become part of Bushy Park in the early seventeenth century.

We know more about the size of Hampton from the Hearth Tax returns of the seventeenth century when buildings were taxed depending on the number of hearths they contained. The return for 1664 shows that Hampton town had 18 one-hearth dwellings, 26 with two hearths, 22 with three or four hearths, 9 with five or six, and 11 with seven. For Hampton Wick the corresponding figures were 14, 19, 14, 7 and 7; additionally one, John Harris, is recorded as having 20 hearths. The parish constable for Hampton Wick, Edward Hancock, put himself down for two hearths, but his successor noted that Hancock actually had five and he was called to account for it.

As in other villages the administration of the area was divided between the manorial courts which retained management of agriculture and the tenanting of land and property, and the parish whose power grew gradually after the Poor Law Act of 1601 imposed the provision of poor relief on parishes.

*18. The heart of Hampton village in c1860 – Red Lion Square.*

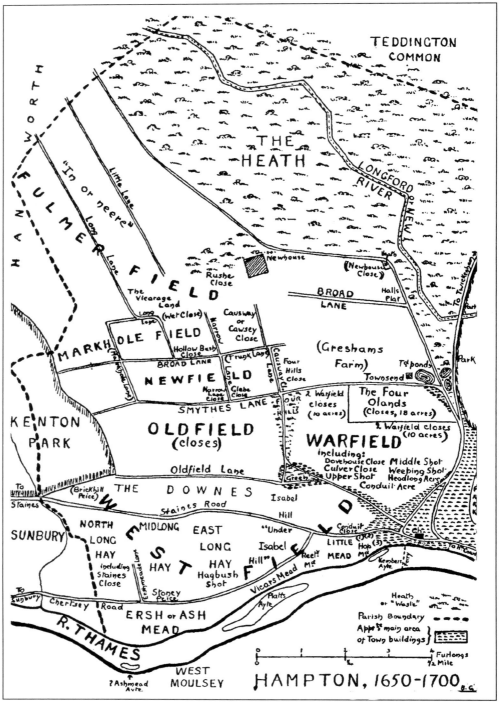

19. *Field map of Hampton 1650-1700. This map, drawn by Bernard Garside, who wrote a series of ten books on Hampton in the sixteenth and seventeenth centuries, shows a reconstructed map of the fields and lanes of Hampton 'town' as they would have been at that time. Many of these lanes are still followed by the modern road pattern.*

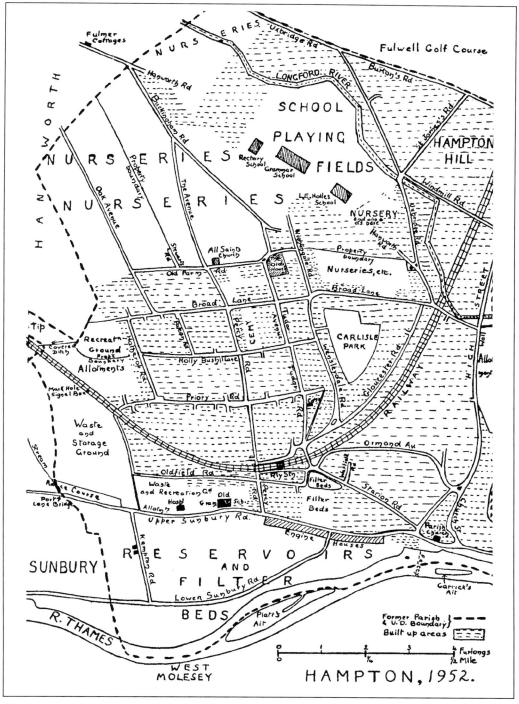

20. *This map, drawn by Bernard Garside in 1952, is the companion map to the seventeenth century one on the previous page. For the sake of clarity, it does not include all the side roads. It shows very distinctly how many modern roads in Hampton follow old lanes and field boundaries.*

The parish management consisted of two church-wardens, a constable, an overseer of the poor and a surveyor of highways, all elected from the residents and all unpaid. The responsibilities of the church-wardens included the upkeep of parish property such as the church and burial ground, and also the doling out of charities.

Hampton parish meetings were at first held in the church, but later in the more convivial surroundings of the Feathers, or the Shipp or the Bell, though the Feathers, which was parish-owned, was the favourite.

The churchwardens' accounts reveal the visit in 1670 of the 'King's Surveyor' (most likely Sir Christopher Wren) who viewed the church and measured it in preparation for the building of a new steeple, which was completed in 1679. In the accounts for 1678-9 Mrs Fall, landlady of the Shipp, was paid £1.12.0d for a dinner for Wren and a Captain Rider. Six new church bells, with new frames, were installed at the time and these lasted until the demolition of the

21. *A view of the village of Hampton from the Surrey bank, 1827. Artist unknown.*

old church in 1830. They also gave their name to the Six Bells, an eighteenth-century building on the site of the present White Hart. It is believed that the church clock, which is known to have been mended in 1651, was either replaced or extensively restored at the time of the tower rebuilding and thus a church clock has been part of Hampton village life for centuries.

The church bells were rung when the King passed through Hampton (usually on his way to Hampton Court Palace from Windsor). This happened six times between April and June in 1684; on these occasions the ringers were paid money for drinks or an account covering all paid occasions was run up for them at one of the nearby inns. In 1688 Goody Bosworth of the Feathers received £2.4.6d and in 1691 the 'drink drunke by the ringers' cost £1.14.6d.

Other miscellaneous items in the accounts include amounts spent on going to nearby fairs to buy a parish bull. After the 1667 purchase a further 6d had to be spent 'for [de]bugging the bull'!

*22. The Lord Mayor of London's barge at Hampton. By Thomas Rowlandson, c.1800.*

The older buildings of Hampton clustered round the church. These included three notable inns. In Thames Street, by the junction of Church Street, still stands what was formerly The Feathers inn (now divided into three cottages) built *c*.1540. Next door is the vicarage (built 1883), but it is at least the third vicarage on the site – a 'curate house' is mentioned in deeds of 1655 which was probably an earlier form. The Bell was rebuilt in 1893 after a fire a year earlier had destroyed what was probably an early sixteenth-century building. The Red Lion (earlier called The Shipp), was certainly in business in 1661. The present building, converted to offices, was erected in 1909, again after a fire in 1908. In this case, however, the fire had been started deliberately and used as practice for the fire brigade, since the building was due for redevelopment anyway. A movie film of this event survives to this day. These three inns are dealt with in greater detail on p101.

A number of substantial buildings were built in what is now Church Street and High Street in the seventeenth century. These included the Old Grange in Church Street, which still stands, and the manor house (Manor Gardens mark its location) which was noted in the 1664 Hearth Tax return as having 13 hearths. This was replaced in the eighteenth century by a building which itself gave way to the present development in 1935-6. Another, more isolated, building was Newhouse (which had seven hearths in 1664) and was later called the Old Farmhouse – this stood in Old Farm Road.

On the Hampton Court Road by the river were St Alban's (demolished 1972), The Cedars (now called Garrick's Lodge), and a large house on the site of today's Garrick's Villa.

Closer to Hampton Court still stands the large brick block called the Royal Mews, which includes a sixteenth-century barn. These buildings were probably begun by Wolsey and enlarged by Henry VIII. The main part was built mid sixteenth century, but has been altered since. The Cardinal Wolsey pub stands on the site of an old barn.

Near the then ferry dock at Hampton Court stood two inns in the seventeenth century. One was the Mitre, on the up-river side of the later bridge. The other, on the down-river side roughly opposite today's Mitre, was the Toye Inn, which was probably built in the reign of Henry VIII, and at which the Toye Club met – its president was the future William IV. The Toye was demolished in 1857 and the site is now a green plot outside the Palace wall, immediately south of the Trophy Gates. By the Lion Gates of the Palace stands the King's Arms, a successor of a seventeenth-century building.

There was also a Shipp at Hampton Wick and a King's Head. Other seventeenth-century inns at the Wick included the Black Dog, the White Hart; the Swan, which still survives in a modern building, was trading in the sixteenth century. From the same period is the so-called 'Wolsey's Cottage' in Lower Teddington Road.

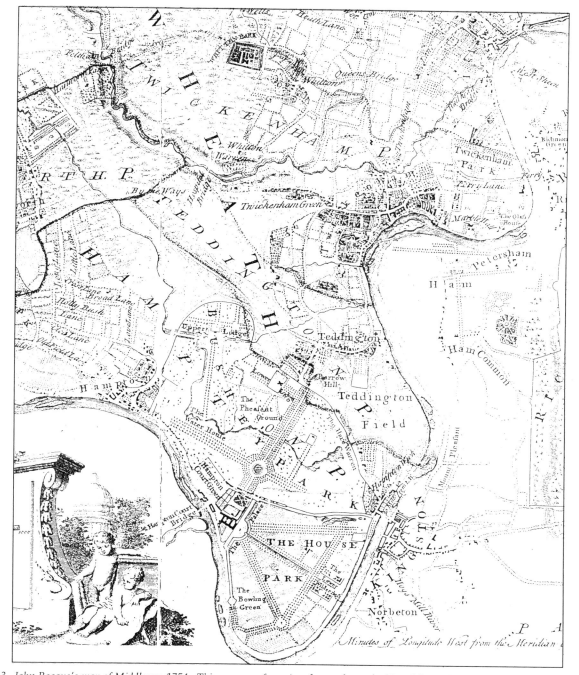

23. *John Rocque's map of Middlesex, 1754. This was one of a series of maps drawn by him of the environs of London. For many towns, they provide the first detailed map, and whilst there are a few earlier maps of Teddington, these are incomplete and relate to specific estates only.*

*The map shown above is an updated version of his 1745-6 map and the scale still shows the distinct villages of Hampton, Hampton Wick and Teddington. Hampton Court Palace is shown as an imposing area at the bottom of the map. Note the avenues of trees in Bushy Park and Home (House on the map) Park – some of their planting pattern survives.*

## TEDDINGTON

Teddington contained some very large houses in the seventeenth century, judging by the same Hearth Tax returns. William Hill, the lord of the manor, was taxed for 18 hearths, Sir Orlando Bridgeman for 17, and Elizabeth Hart for 15.

The village of Teddington grew up around the old parish church by the river, at the corner of High Street and Twickenham Road; a manor house stood off the road, opposite the church, and there was a village pond at the corner of Park Street.

The Teddington manorial estate was run on a day-to-day basis by a reeve, who reported to Westminster Abbey's bailiff before the Dissolution and generally to the Crown's bailiff afterwards. The Court Leet met twice a year to deal with disputes, and it also appointed a manorial constable, beadle, rent collector and two ale-tasters.

The parish vestry began to exercise greater influence in the area in the eighteenth century. This was probably because of the activities of their long-serving vicar, Dr Stephen Hales. In 1767 a Vestry Room was built under the tower of St Mary's church to avoid holding their meetings in local inns.

Teddington was particularly concerned to deter poor strangers entering the parish where they might become a charge on the poor rate. To this end gates were erected on the main roads into the village and these were manned by the poor to work off part of their subsidy. There were six gates and although their whereabouts is unknown, they were recorded as by the manor house, the church gate, opposite the stile close to Hampton Wick, the gate at Benjamin Watts, the gate that opens to the lane by Mr Fry's, and at the upper end of the street near the common.

## DANGEROUS TIMES

Despite this tightening of security against the itinerant poor Teddington at times was an unsafe place. At Easter in 1710 a group of young men came from Twickenham to 'secure' the maypole, which stood somewhere between the King's Head and Queen Elizabeth's Hunting Lodge. The maypole was defended by some Teddington lads and in the ensuing fight one of them, John Rolt, was struck on the head and killed. Two of the Twickenham youths were arrested and taken to Newgate. Sir Charles Duncombe, of Teddington Place, directed the jury at the coroner's inquest to bring in a charge of murder but at their trial at the Old Bailey insufficient evidence was offered and the men were acquitted. Ironically, the maypole was found rotting in the churchyard some years later.

The actress, Kitty Clive, wrote to David Garrick in 1776: 'I have been robbed and murdered coming from Kingston, Jimy [her brother] and I in a postchey at half past nine, just by Teddington Church. I only lost a little silver and my senses, for one of them came into the carriage with a great horsepistol to 'sarch' me for my watch, but I had not it with me.'

In July 1785 the Rev. John Cosens (vicar of Teddington) and his wife were returning home from dinner with Horace Walpole when they were held up by highwaymen almost at the gates to Strawberry Hill. Walpole wrote to a friend advising this and adding 'it is agreeable to have banditi on one's doorstep.'

In 1793 the Teddington parish cage was built for the containment of disorderly persons. This was in Park Lane and probably near the parish stocks. It was popularly held that when the village drunks were locked up, they would cajole the occupants of the almshouses to supply them with more drink dispensed to them by a spout of a teapot through the bars of the cage window.

*24. Kitty Clive.*

# Hampton Court Palace

Hampton Court Palace is a building of national importance and one of the finest Tudor buildings in the land. Since it is the subject of many dozens of books, it is not within the scope of this volume to dwell at length on its history and features. However, a brief summary will be given of the history of some of the more notable aspects of the building that the visitor may see nowadays.

Cardinal Thomas Wolsey, who took over the lease of Hampton Court from the Knights Hospitaller of the Order of St John of Jerusalem in 1514, built much of the Palace that survives today. Henry VIII who by 1529 had 'acquired' it from Wolsey, greatly extended the building. However, much of Henry's work, including the King's and Queen's lodgings, was demolished in 1689-91 to be replaced by the Royal Apartments, built by Sir Christopher Wren. There have been subsequent alterations to the Palace, which was opened to the public by Queen Victoria in 1838.

As a general summary, the main features were built at the following times:

25. *General topography of Hampton Court parks and meadows, HamptonWick and the river, before the changes in the reigns of Charles II and William III.*

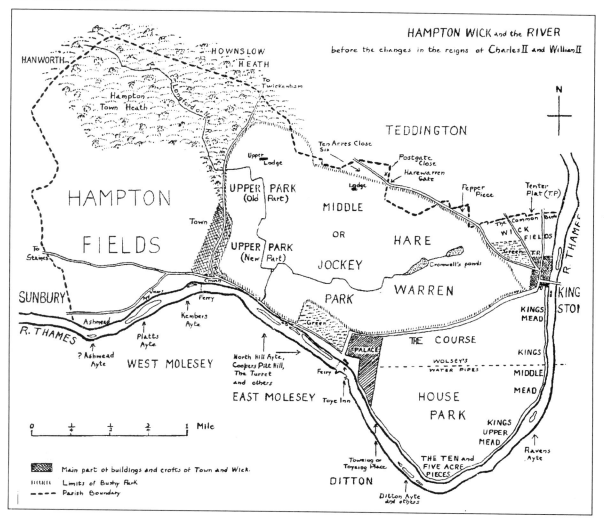

*Base Court, chapel and part of kitchens* (Wolsey 1514-29);

*Great Hall, Lord Chamberlain's Court, part of kitchens and Chapel Court* (Henry VIII 1529-47);

*Fountain Court, East Front, South Front, King's and Queen's Apartments, Orangery* (William and Mary, designed by Wren 1689-1702);

*George II Gateway, East side of Clock Court* (designed by William Kent).

It is just possible that one or two fragments of building from pre-Wolsey survive in the interior of the palace, and that the chapel built by Wolsey is on the site of that used by the Knights Hospitaller.

## THE WEST FRONT

The usual approach to the Palace is through the Trophy Gates towards the West Front and Great Gate House. Although Wolsey's Great Gate House was reduced from five to three storeys during 1771-3 and refaced with new bricks in the 1880s, it still presents a view that would have been familiar to its builder. However, this was not always the case, and the view has changed substantially over this century, being now much closer to its original appearance. A hundred years ago there was no visible moat or moat bridge with its now familiar 'King's Beasts' guarding the bridge, along the parapets. The moat had been filled in around 1689 and the Tudor bridge (built 1535), was buried in the process. It was not until 1872 when drainage work was being carried out that some old stonework was accidentally located. This was soon covered up, but meanwhile it had been seen by Ernest Law, the Hampton Court historian, who later

27. *A procession of boats accompanying Charles II and Queen Catherine from Whitehall to Hampton Court in 1662.*

correctly conjectured that this must have been the Tudor moat bridge. An excavation was conducted in 1909-10 in which the moat bridge was located about three feet below the ground, together with the bases of the octagonal shafts that had risen above the parapet, and which formerly carried the heraldic beasts that had been carved in 1536. Originally there had been twelve King's Beasts but to-day there are only ten. This is due to the fact that the gatehouse had been altered and rebuilt in 1773 and there was no longer room to replace two of the beasts in their original

26. *The east front of Hampton Court. This view, published in 1780, is particularly interesting as it shows the Palace 'as finished by K. Henry VII [sic]'. It thus shows the East Front before the rebuilding by Wren from 1689 onwards. Apart from the Tennis Court on the right hand side and the Great Hall also visible on the right, almost everything shown here has been replaced.*

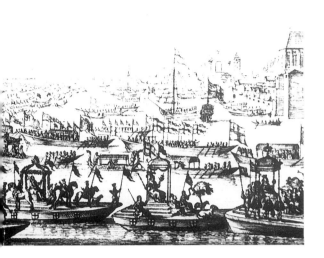

## THE ASTRONOMICAL CLOCK

After passing through the Great Gatehouse and across Base Court, the next courtyard is Clock Court. This contains the Astronomical Clock built by Nicholas Oursian in 1540. Nowadays little of the clock's workings are original except for the dial. This consists of three concentric copper discs of different sizes that indicate the position of the sun, phases of the moon and other information as well as the time.

## THE GREAT HALL AND THE CHAPEL ROYAL

Built in 1532-5, the Great Hall is 106 feet long, 40 feet wide and 60 feet high. It contains one of the most magnificent Tudor roofs in the country, and is of the hammer-beam type. The stained-glass windows were restored in 1840-6. The tapestries on the walls were commissioned by Henry VIII in the late 1520s.

The best Tudor ceiling in the country is, however, in the Chapel Royal. It was built in 1535-6 and resembles a stone fan-vaulted ceiling although it is actually made from wood. The decoration and intricate carving are simply stunning. The large wooden panel behind the reredos was carved by Grinling Gibbons in the reign of Queen Anne. It obscures the former East Window, the tracery of which survives behind the panel. The Royal Pew at the west end of the Chapel replaced the previous Tudor gallery at the time of Queen Anne.

positions. The beasts that were placed there in 1911 only lasted until 1950 when new ones were carved.

Thus the moat and moat bridge which had been invisible for around 220 years were restored to close their original appearance.

*28. A photograph of the Trophy Gates, looking towards the west front, in the 1860s.*

29. *Excavation of the old bridge over the old moat in 1909.*

30. *The Astronomical Clock.*

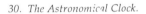

31. *Interior of the Chapel Royal*

## THE TUDOR KITCHENS

These were built by Wolsey and extended by Henry, although small fragments have been found in excavation which may relate to an earlier kitchen on the site (probably a timber-framed building) of the Knights Hospitaller. The demands on the kitchens were enormous. The Great Hall sat about 300 people and there had to be two sittings for meals as about 600 people were entitled to eat there. In addition, the Lord Steward's department had a staff of up to 200 people, most of whom ate in the Great Kitchen.

After the kitchens were enlarged by Henry, they comprised over fifty rooms covering 36,000 square feet. They included wet, dry and flesh larders, pastry house, boiling house, saucery, spicery and buttery.

## THE ROYAL APARTMENTS

There is insufficient room to describe these in any kind of detail. Both the King's and Queen's apartments were built in the period 1689-1700. The King's were badly affected by the disastrous fire of 1986, but have now been restored. Both sets of apartments have magnificent staircases leading up to them, in the case of the King's staircase the walls and ceiling were painted by Verrio.

Sir Christopher Wren was commissioned in 1689 to remodel the palace for William and Mary. It was intended to demolish all of the Tudor palace except the Great Hall. This was to be the centre of a new northern approach, formed by Chestnut Avenue, in Bushy Park, sweeping around the Diana Fountain and entering the Palace on the northern side. In the event, although Chestnut Avenue was planted in 1699, the scheme as far as the northern facade of the Palace was concerned was never completed.

Initially huge sums of money were made available as the monarchs were anxious to see the results. Later, after workmen had been killed and injured in a collapse of a large section of the south range, the work was undertaken at a less frenetic pace and with more care. It stopped altogether in 1694 with the death of Mary, who had been the great advocate of the scheme. In 1698, after fire destroyed Whitehall Palace, Wren was asked for an estimate for completion, although in the event a lower estimate by his deputy, William Talman, was accepted.

Furniture began arriving in 1699, and between 1700 and his death in 1702 William spent most of the year at Hampton Court. After her accession Anne stayed occasionally using the King's Apartments as the Queen's Apartments were still unfinished. Later George I and II had occasional holidays here, but the King's Apartments were not used by a reigning monarch after the 1730s.

*32. The Great Kitchen in 1909, built in the time of Cardinal Wolsey.*

Cardinal Wolsey's Kitchen, Hampton Court Palace.

106

33. *The south-east front, designed by Wren. Photograph of c.1860.*

## THE GARDENS

Although the overall layout of the gardens dates from Henry VIII's time what exists to-day bears little relationship to a Tudor garden.

The two best-known features are the Great Vine and the Maze. The Great Vine was planted in 1768 and has in the past produced more than 2,000lbs of grapes in a year, although fewer bunches are nowadays allowed to grow to maturity. The world-famous Maze was planted in the 1690s and contains walks totalling over half a mile.

On 6 July 1995 the newly restored Privy (Private) Garden was opened to the public by Prince Charles. This garden on the south (river) side of the Palace was originally laid out in 1702 in the time of William III. It was intended to be overlooked by the then newly-constructed King's Apartments designed by Wren. The garden was a Parterre – intricately patterned with cut turf bordered by low box hedging and flower beds called 'Plattes Bondes'. These were planted with clipped yews and hollies, standard shrubs and herbacious plants such as honeysuckle and lavender. After 1760 the garden entered a period of decline and by 1993 had become an overgrown shrubbery. A programme to restore the garden began that year, taking more than two years to complete.

The garden now restored to its original layout will once again complement the King's Apartments (which themselves were restored after the 1986 fire).

34. *Skating on the Long Water, c.1905.*

35. *Aerial view of Hampton Court Maze, with the King's Arms in the foreground.*

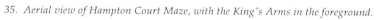

36.  *The first Hampton Court Bridge.  This was opened in 1753 and replaced a ferry that then existed.  It was of very frail construction with seven steep-sided wooden arches, and lasted only 25 years.*

# Crossing the River

Jurisdiction over the Thames from the Medway to Staines was in the hands of the City of London from 1197 to 1857 – ownership was also claimed by the City but disputed by the Crown. However, the Thames Conservancy Act was passed in 1857 and a Board of Conservancy established which still included representatives from the Corporation. This was a short-lived body and the Thames Conservancy Board replaced it in 1866 with powers over the whole river from Cricklade. This Board remained in control until the Port of London Authority was established in 1909, with jurisdiction over the river from the tidal limit at Teddington down to the sea, leaving the old Board the remainder of the tideless river. This arrangement was again changed in 1974 when the Thames Water Authority took over the responsibilities of both the Authority and the Board.

The Thames has not always been the navigable river we know today. It had many shallows, there were stakes and other obstructions used in connection with fishing, and water extraction to power mills caused problems with water-levels.

Things changed as from 1770 when the lock system of the upper Thames was developed.

Originally locks were 'flash locks', that had only one gate and when opened caused a flash or flush of water to be released enabling at least temporary navigation, as well as the flotation of any barges or

*37. The Anglers pub and the Teddington ferry. Although not as famous as its Twickenham neighbour, the Teddington ferry operated until about 1950 from the public drawdock to the Surrey bank and to Lock Island after the lock was built.*

38. *Teddington weir and lock. The weir was first mentioned in 1345. The first lock was built in 1811 and has been rebuilt and enlarged several times since.*

39. *'A view of Hampton Court ferry from my lodgings - 1739'. This drawing shows the ferry, as well as a horse-drawn cart, fording the river before the first bridge was built. The ferry had been in existence since at least 1536.*

other craft that had become grounded. Unfortunately, this method also left the river very low indeed after the wall of water had been released.

Pound locks, of the sort we know today, were developed with two gates, which released only a lock-full of water. The one at Teddington was built in 1811 and that at Molesey (just upstream of Hampton Court Bridge) was opened in 1815.

## BRIDGES ACROSS

Bridges also constituted a navigational hazard. There was a wooden bridge between Kingston and Hampton Wick from around 1219, which was probably instrumental in the development of a settlement at Hampton Wick. The bridge had fifteen piers, not very far apart and the present structure, with much wider arches, replaced it in 1828.

The residents of Hampton itself made do at first with a ford where Hampton Court Bridge now is, particularly used in the drier season. There were also two ferries – one that crossed the river on the line of the bridge from at least 1536, and another which docked near St Mary's church.

The first, highly decorative, bridge at Hampton Court was opened in 1753. It was a frail construction built on seven steep-sided arches, which lasted only 25 years. Its replacement, also of wood, was opened in 1778. This was 350 feet long, 18 feet wide and had ten arches raised on piles, with a toll house on the Middlesex side. It was a sturdier bridge than its

predecessor, but it was pulled down in 1864 and during the construction of a new one on the same line, traffic was ferried across the river.

The third bridge, opened in 1865, was made of wrought-iron lattice girders in five spans resting on four pairs of octagonal cast-iron columns which were sunk 16 feet into the river bed and on brick abutments. Remains of the abutments survive to this day and can be seen on both sides of the river. There was a brick toll house on the Middlesex side which is nowadays incorporated as part of the Mitre hotel. Tolls ceased in 1876 and the posts of the old tollgate were transferred to outside St Mary's church, where they may still be seen.

With the increase of traffic, especially on race-days at Hurst Park or on Hampton Court fair days, a new bridge, the one we see today, was built. Construction began in 1930, slightly downstream from the old line. This meant the demolition of the Castle Hotel which had stood on the Molesey side of the river since about 1620, the pulling down of wooden bridges which had connected with Hampton Court station, the diversion of the rivers Mole and Ember, and the construction of a new approach road connecting with the Portsmouth Road.

The new bridge, designed in collaboration with Sir Edwin Lutyens, was built of ferro-concrete and is faced with red brick and Portland stone in the Wren style. It has three arches and the road is 40 feet wide with two footpaths each of 15 feet. It was officially opened by the Prince of Wales on 3 July 1933.

*40. The second Hampton Court bridge in 1864.*

41.  *The third Hampton Court bridge c.1905*

42.  *The present Hampton Court bridge at the time of its construction in 1933 alongside its predecessor. From the* Morning Post, *10 March 1933*

# Islands in the River

The stretch of river at Hampton and Teddington contained many islands, usually known as aits or eyots: this is a word which has found its way into several place names along the Thames such as Bermondsey, Molesey and Chertsey. The number of these islands has declined over the years with improvements to navigation. Confusingly, apart from appearing and disappearing with the state of the river, many have had name alterations due to a change of ownership.

Of the islands which exist today Platt's Eyot is one of the largest. It is now the base for the River Police and houses some light industry. Up to around 1884 it had been used for growing osiers. In 1888 an intake for the filter beds on the adjacent waterworks was formed on the island and between 1898 and 1901 further filter beds were constructed and the excavated soil dumped on the island, raising its level considerably.

Platt's also housed the firm of Immisch & Co., boatbuilders, who marketed a famous range of electric canoes and launches. Later the firm was taken over by Thornycroft's and fast naval craft were built; all the firm's boatbuilding operation has now been transferred to Southampton.

*44. The Immisch launch, built on Platt's Eyot.*

*43. Trowlock Island, early this century.*

45.  *Benn's boathouse, reputed to have been built before 1704, at 5-9 Thames Street before being demolished in 1946-7.  Nearby Benn's Al-*
*between 1 and 3 Thames Street, still commemorates the name of this old-established boatbuilding yard.*

Downstream from Platt's Eyot, near Hampton ferry, is Benn's Eyot, a tiny island completed covered by Hampton Sailing Club; it is connected by a chain ferry to the shore at the end of Benn's Alley. The name Benn derives from an old established boatbuilding business – its old boathouse, reputed to be built before 1704, was demolished in 1946-7.

Then comes Garrick's Ait, just downstream from St Mary's church. This was once known as Shanko's Eyot. The level of this island was also raised by soil excavated for the Waterworks at the end of the last century. For many years it was used for camping and picnicking and there were no permanent buildings, but later plots were rented and buildings appeared. Formerly, there was a very small island at the eastern end of the ait, which diminished in size over many years and the remains were finally removed during dredging in 1947.

The next tiny island, sometimes known as Duck's Eyot, is at the head of Tagg's Island and has room for little more than a resting place for ducks and waterfowl. The much more substantial and well-known Tagg's Island was earlier known as Walnut Tree Island. Nowadays it is home to many houseboats, both around the edge of the island and in the central lagoon that was dredged in the early 1980s. It is connected to the Middlesex bank via an arched bridge that replaced one built in the last war to facilitate production of munitions on the island.

In the 1850s there was a ramshackle beerhouse here called the Anglers Retreat. In 1868 Tom Tagg moved to the island where he established a boatbuilding business, and in 1872 he took over the lease of the pub and built the Island Hotel. The business fell away after his death and the island was leased to Fred Karno, the well-known impresario, who opened The Karsino here in 1913. This was a most luxurious complex. It had a vehicle ferry on the Middlesex side and a passenger ferry to the Surrey bank. it was initially very popular, but the First World War intervened and it was never the same again, despite subsequent name changes to the Thames Riviera, the Palm Beach and The Casino. In 1940 A.C. Cars moved to the island and the first bridge was built to Hampton Court Road – the present bridge replaced it in 1982. The hotel itself was demolished in 1971 and after many development proposals and years of wrangling the centre of the island was excavated in 1983 to create a lagoon for mooring houseboats.

Immediately below Tagg's Island is Ash Island, which had previously been known as Harvey's island and before that Garrick's Lower Eyot (Garrick was a one-time tenant). Harvey built an Anglers Retreat on this island before transferring it to Tagg's Island, mainly to avoid flooding. The headquarters of Molesey Boat Club, founded in 1866, were initially on this island, although they later moved to the Surrey bank.

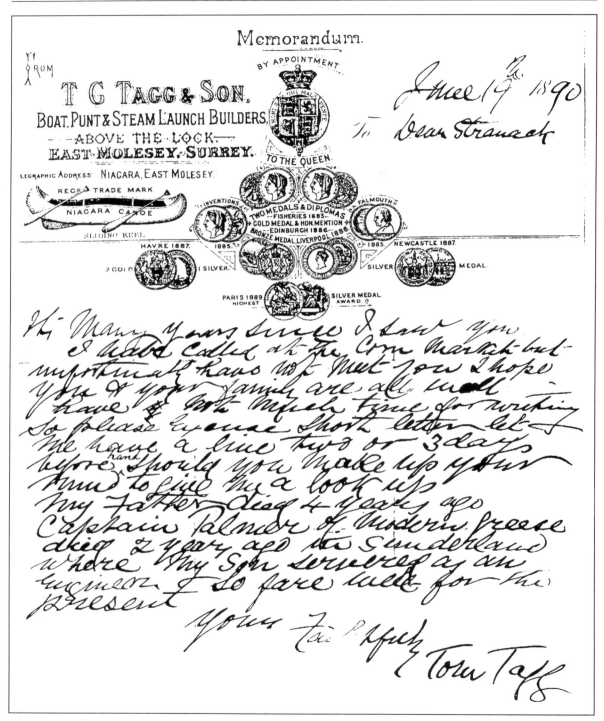

46.  *Letter signed by Tom Tagg, of Tagg's Island, 1890.*

47. *The Karsino, owned by Fred Karno on Tagg's Island*

48. *Interior of the Karsino.*

49. *Demolition of the Karsino, Tagg's Island in 1971*

Molesey weir, originally built in 1815, extends from Ash Island to the Middlesex bank.

The weir, lock, bridge and other views in this stretch of river have all been recorded by Alfred Sisley, perhaps one of the lesser-known but still important Impressionists. He made seventeen paintings in 1874 of the short stretch of river between just below Hampton Court Bridge and Hampton.

In 1502 there is mention of Creweyte in Teddington but nobody seems to know exactly where this was.

Steven's Aits were first referred to in 1362 as 'an eyte in the water of the Thames'. Perhaps it was only one island then. It consists now of two small islands, the biggest of which is 200ft long and 20ft wide. At the end of the eighteenth century, a paygate was established on the towpath for the City of London to apply a toll on the tonnage of barges passing this point.

Steven's Aits, which take their name from a nineteenth-century boatman who lived on the site of Boaters public house and supplied an osier crop to the City each year. The islands were never big enough to encourage much occupation and the last known inhabitant was John Kemp, who was caretaker of the islands for over 30 years. In the nineteenth century

the main island was also known as Tatham's Island and sometimes Tea Pot Island and was a popular picnicking site amongst the boating fraternity.

With Kingston Rowing Club opposite and with their banks reinforced by concrete pilings, they now provide a haven for wildfowl who nest in the willow trees.

Further downstream is Trowlock Island which takes its name from a trow – a type of Thames barge capable of taking loads of 50-60 tons. It sits near the Lensbury Club and is connected to the mainland by a chain ferry. There are many chalet bungalows here although in Stanford's opinion they 'do nothing for the view; they and similar ticky-tacky will be a blot on the landscape to Staines.'

This was where Harry Gibbs set up his boatbuilding business in 1910, which was to continue until 1940. Also around 1910, the Royal Canoe Club was founded here and still flourishes today.

At the time of the construction of the lock in 1811, a lock cut was inserted on the Surrey bank and this created Lock Island, reached by the suspension bridge from the Teddington side.

# Houseboats and Regattas

## HOUSEBOATS

The Hampton stretch of river was a very popular base for houseboats, mainly due to the ease with which it could be reached by train – the railway had arrived at Hampton Court in 1849 and Hampton in 1864. The houseboats, mainly used as weekend retreats or during the summer for holidays, were clustered around Tagg's Island with more just below the bridge on the Surrey side.

Names such as *River Dream, Astoria, Satsuma* and *Gipsy* were once well known throughout the area. Many of these craft were of massive proportions, beautifully decorated and festooned with plants and flowers, particularly during regatta times and, lit with lanterns at night, they were a magnificent sight lining the island banks.

*The Wildflower* was 110 feet in length and the *Astoria* 92 feet; the latter is now moored at Garrick's Lawn slightly upriver from her original mooring. No expense was spared on the *Astoria* by the man who had her built – Fred Karno. It was used for entertaining, to impress people, and also for what are nowadays known as 'casting-couch' purposes. The cabins were panelled in solid mahogany and the bathroom walled and fitted with marble. The sun deck, over which there was a magnificent wrought-iron framework, was illuminated by hundreds of lamps, and would often have an orchestra playing on it.

The houseboats below the bridge were given notice to quit in 1931 due to the imminent construction of the new bridge and the diversion of the rivers Mole and Ember. The *Astoria* was towed upriver to her present mooring place in 1951, when a later owner wanted more privacy than could be had on Tagg's Island.

Several of the houseboats still moored at Tagg's hark back to more splendid days. The newer craft, whilst not as grand as their forbears, continue a tradition that has a long local history.

## REGATTAS

A number of regattas have been held on the stretch of river between Hampton and Molesey for many years, the best-known being the Molesey Amateur Regatta held in July. This was founded in 1867 and is still held. In 1883 this event was described as 'in the opinion of many capable of judging it holds second place to Henley Regatta alone, to which, in fact, it bids fair to become a formidable rival'. For many years the grounds of Garrick Temple (then in private hands as part of the Garrick estate) were used as the committee lawn for the Molesey regatta. Later the course and

50. *The Gipsy houseboat at Hampton.*

51.  *The Sans Souci houseboat.*

52.  *The Cigarette, a 'Floating Palace' owned by Dr Walford Bodie, moored near The Lawns, Thames Ditton, opposite Hampton Court Palace.*

53. *Regatta Day at Molesey, 1909.*

54. *The fashions of the day at Molesey Regatta in 1907.*

*55. Yachting at Teddington. From the 1880s boating became a very popular pastime on this stretch of river.*

*56. Molesey Regatta Day c1905.*

committee lawn were moved to the Surrey side which, apart from a short-lived reversion to Hampton, have remained there since.

An older event was what was originally called the Watermen's regatta, held in August, first run in 1835 and discontinued after 1910. This annual event was much more of an entertainment, with water jousting, canoe polo etc.

There have been other regattas of a more local nature. One was called Hampton regatta, a descendant of the Watermen's event, and police rowing club regattas were held in the 1890s.

*57. The Teddington Gates of Bushy Park.*

# Bushy Park

### A HUNTING PLACE

At about 1,100 acres Bushy Park is the second largest Royal Park in London. At one time it was connected to Hounslow Heath, but it is not clear when it was first emparked. The Knights Hospitaller probably used it, but certainly when Cardinal Wolsey leased the manor of Hampton from them he lost no time in extending the estate and in 1514 he enclosed the old sheep pasture of 'Hamntone'. When Henry VIII acquired the Wolsey estate he stocked the park with deer and game and divided it into three by means of brick walls: Upper Park, the area to the north of Hampton, Middle Park, south of Bushy House to Hampton Court Green, and the Harewarren, east of Chestnut Avenue. The whole of the park was walled around by 1540. At the same time, he was also creating a Chase on areas of land on the south of the river in Molesey, Walton, Esher, Weybridge, Thames Ditton and Shepperton.

Elizabeth I shared her father's love of hunting and was a frequent visitor to the Palace, though her preference was for Richmond Palace. James I followed her at Hampton, though some historians have complained that he cheated at hunting, creeping up on grazing deer under cover of trees so as to shoot them at close range.

The main change during the reign of Charles I was the creation of the Longford river, which diverted water from the River Colne. This waterway, sometimes called Cardinal's, Queen's or King's river, is eleven miles long, but was constructed with remarkable speed – from October 1638 until completion in July 1639 – at a cost of £4,100. It runs from Longford on the Colne, past Hanworth, through Bushy Park and thence to Hampton Court where it supplies the ornamental waters.

After the execution of Charles I, Hampton Court and Bushy Park were sold by auction in 1653. Cromwell, however, when he was appointed Lord Protector of the Commonwealth, acquired both the Palace and Bushy Park for his official residence and it was in this period that the Longford river was diverted into some new ponds which were dug on the Harewarren. These were once known as Oliver's or Cromwell's ponds, but today one of them is called Heron Pond, possibly a corruption of Harewarren.

General George Monck, later to play a prominent part in the restoration of Charles II, was appointed Chief Steward and Ranger in 1659-60, after Cromwell's death and he was confirmed in this post by a grateful Charles II. The new monarch commenced a tree planting programme of Dutch lime trees, and created the Long Water. Edward Proger built a lodge in the Middle Park, possibly to provide a venue for Charles' many liaisons, and also the first Bushy House. He was

58. *The Diana Fountain.*

appointed Keeper of the Middle Park in 1665, a position he held for 48 years until his death at the age of 96 caused 'of the anguish of cutting four new teeth'. He was buried in Hampton church and his tombstone was recently discovered beneath the lectern.

William and Mary took to Hampton Court – the flat land around reminded the king of Holland. To coincide with Wren's remodelling of the Palace, he planned a grand new approach from the Teddington Gate to the north side of the Great Hall. A new road was built, flanked either side by a line of horse-chestnut trees, and a round pond was dug near the Lion Gate, again using water from the Longford river. But it was in the Home Park here where William broke his collarbone after a fall when his horse stumbled on a molehill; he contracted pneumonia and died in 1702. The event gave rise to the Jacobite toast 'to the little gentleman in the black velvet waistcoat'.

Queen Anne found herself financially embarrassed and cut the maintenance of both the Park and its gardens. Leonard Knyff, the artist, wrote to a col-league: 'I have done a great many drawings of Hampton Court and Windsor for his Highness [Anne's husband, Prince George of Denmark] for which I have not been paid!'. At this time the statue in the King's Privy Garden was moved to its present site in the round pond in Bushy Park and from then on the statue became known as Diana.

## RESTRICTED ACCESS

The Earl of Halifax, an eminent minister in Anne's reign, became Keeper of Bushy Park as well as Keeper of Home Park, Steward of Hampton and Keeper of Middle Park and the Harewarren. It was the Earl who rebuilt Bushy House and it was here that his nephew and heir spent much of his time. In 1734 the 2nd Earl commenced the building of a new wall which would completely surround the parks, thereby impeding traditional local footpaths and obliging residents to obtain tickets of entry.

This situation created much resentment, and it was a humble local resident who took the matter to a head. Timothy Bennett was a cordwainer or shoemaker in Hampton Wick and had premises roughly where the car-park of the Swan public house is today. Local tradition holds that Timothy was incensed that villagers had to walk around the walls in order to reach the church at Hampton, or else, because of the closure of the footpath fewer people walked past his shop, leading to a reduction of trade.

Having briefed an attorney, he was summoned to see Earl Halifax and explain why he should 'meddle in this affair'. Bennett replied: 'I remember, an't please your lordship, to have seen, when I was a young man, sitting at work, the people cheerfully pass my shop to Kingston market; but now, my lord, they are forced to go round about, through a hot sandy road, ready to faint beneath their burdens, and I am unwilling to leave the world worse than I found it. This, my lord, I humbly represent, is the reason why I have taken this work in hand.'

Halifax dismissed him for being impertinent but did, however, reopen the gate and footpath. Bennett died two years later, aged 77, already a local hero.

This story begs the question as to how a common cordwainer would have the connections and resources to take on the nobility in legal proceedings. By coincidence, a similar case was proceeding in Richmond where John Lewis, a brewer, was suing Princess Amelia, the Ranger of Richmond Park over its closure to the public in 1751. Lewis also won his battle, which in his case did get as far as the law courts. Could some anonymous benefactor have financed both men to take on the establishment?

The footpath in Bushy Park is now known as Cobblers Way and in 1900 J.C. Buckmaster opened a mezzotint memorial to Timothy Bennett at the Sandy Lane end.

59. *The chestnut trees in Bushy Park. From the* Illustrated London News, *13 May 1871.*

The offices held by the Halifax family reverted to the Crown in 1771. It was the intention of George III to reward Lord North, a grandson of the first Earl Halifax, with the Rangership, but there was then a Parliamentary rule that a serving minister could not profit from a Crown office. Undeterred, George gave the position instead to North's wife, Lady Anne. North, best remembered as the Prime Minister who lost the American colonies, lived at Bushy House every summer until 1782 when he resigned, and almost continuously thereafter until his death.

Horace Walpole was a frequent dinner guest at the North household. He records that in 1787: 'Lord North's spirits, good humour, wit, sense, drollery are as perfect as ever – the unremitting attention of Lady North and his children most touching; Mr North leads him about [North by then was blind], Miss North sits constantly by him, carves his meat, watches every motion, scarce puts a bit into her own lips.... if ever a loss of sight could be compensated, it is by so affectionate a family.'

North is commemorated in Teddington by North Lane and also gave his name to the North Arms which later became the Guildford Arms and later still the Clarence Arms and Clarence Hotel.

## THE CLARENCES

When Lady North died in 1797 George III was able to find a home for his third son, William, who had left the Navy and was living in Richmond with Mrs Jordan and six of their children – two of their own and four others from previous relationships.

William was always short of money and indulged in a great deal of tree felling to sell the timber. This policy virtually denuded the Park of trees in some areas.

Mrs Jordan was cast aside in 1811 and in 1818 he married Adelaide whom William, when he became king, made Ranger of Bushy Park. As Queen Dowager she lived at Bushy House until her death in 1849.

Shortly after her coronation Queen Victoria opened the picture galleries and gardens of Hampton Court to the public. As a result many out-of-town visitors also came to Bushy Park, a trend accentuated when the London & South Western Railway extended to Hampton Court in 1849. In particular they came to see the annual Chestnut Sunday celebration in the Park.

Teddington Cricket Club, which had lost its old ground to the railway, had a pitch in the park. Horse riding was also permitted after 1885, and some organised shooting was held. One of the local newspapers

60.  *Royal Chestnut Sunday in 1909.*

61.  *A Bicycle meet in Bushy Park. Between 1874 and 1886, the park was a venue for bicycling clubs with a record number of 2,360 cyclists participating in 1882.*

AFTER THE HURRICANE
IN BUSHY PARK
SHOWING DAMAGE
TO LODGE

*62. After the storm in Bushy Park in 1908.*

remarked upon one of the German nobility staying at Hampton Court: 'Baron von Pawel Remmingen has a notion that Bushy Park is a large game reserve kept up by a charitable and benevolent nation for his particular enjoyment and is under the delusion that he can order 'shtrangers' out of the Park if it so suits him.'

The most popular organised sport was the Bicycle Meet. For a short period from 1874 to 1886, Bushy Park was the venue for a gathering of bicycle clubs. From here cyclists would ride through Hampton, Hampton Hill and Teddington and back to the Park again. Starting modestly at about 200 cycles, it rose to a peak of 2,360 in 1882 with 180 clubs represented. The following year was to be the last for bicycles, with only 500-600 participants. Tricycles took over for another three years but did not achieve the popularity of the two-wheeled machines.

A report of 1877 states that it was only ten years since the first wooden bicycle had been made in England and only seven since iron machines with rubber tyres and spider wheels were introduced by the Coventry Machinists Company. At the 1877 meeting all were of the latter type except one wooden one, which was received with astonishment and laughter!

## STORMS OVER BUSHY

On 1 June 1908 a 'hurricane' swept through Bushy Park and was reported in the *Thames Valley Times*:

'The brief paragraph in yesterday's daily papers was the first intimation most people had of the terrible havoc wrought at the Teddington end of Bushy Park at about five minutes to ten on Monday night by a whirlwind which in a few minutes uprooted no fewer than sixty-one trees, principally limes.... The chestnut trees in The Avenue are not damaged very greatly, only a limb here and there having been broken off, but the limes on the left hand side of The Avenue, on entering through the Teddington Gate, have been uprooted and now lie strewn about the ground, completely spoiling the view of this part of the Park.'

Nearly eighty years later the Great Storm of London did far more damage. On 18 October 1987, so intense was the storm that 1,329 trees were felled then or later in the Park. It took three months to clear the fallen trees from the Waterhouse Woodland Garden alone. Much of the timber from the trees has been used by the Parks Department to make bridges, benches, platforms and fencing.

# Illustrious People

## LEICESTER AND BRIDGEMAN

Several luminaries of the late Tudor and early Stuart period are associated with Teddington. Robert Dudley, Earl of Leicester, wrote to Elizabeth I from the Hunting Lodge in the High Street, and Sir Amias Paulet (1536?-1588), best known as the jailer of Mary, Queen of Scots, took a 40-year lease on the manor in 1582, but there is no evidence he actually lived here. Lord Buckhurst, who was Elizabeth's Chancellor, lived in the manor house until his death in 1608.

Sir Orlando Bridgeman (1606?-1674), a prominent Royalist, managed to avoid imprisonment during the years after the execution of Charles I, and was permitted to practise law, especially in the field of conveyancing, a part of law important at the time with the

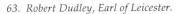

63. *Robert Dudley, Earl of Leicester.*

64. *Sir Orlando Bridgeman, by P. Borssler.*

redistribution of the estates of the Crown and exiled royalists. He had a high legal reputation and was appointed Lord Chief Justice of the Common Pleas in 1660, but he fell from grace when he was Lord Keeper of the Seal and implicated in the plan of Charles II to become a Catholic in return for a subsidy from the French king. So, in 1673 he left office and retired to his house at Teddington, which must have been of some size, judging by the Hearth Tax return, but its location is unknown. He died here and was buried in St Mary's church. During alterations to the church in 1833, his coffin was found open but his body, having been embalmed, was still perfectly preserved, down to his pointed beard; so much so, that his descendant, the Earl of Bradford, was sent for to view the spectacle.

## SIR CHRISTOPHER WREN

Wren (1632-1723) has left a permanent mark on Hampton in that he substantially rebuilt the Palace during the reign of William and Mary. Fountain Court, the King's and Queen's Apartments, the East and South fronts of the building, are all his.

During this work, between 1706-23, he resided on and off at the Old Court House, Hampton Court Green.

# DAVID GARRICK

Garrick (1717-79) was one of the greatest actors to appear on the English stage, particularly famous for his Shakespearian roles – he is buried in Westminster Abbey at the foot of Shakespeare's statue. He also owned and managed at times Drury Lane Theatre, which with a partner he bought in 1747 and retained until his retirement in 1766.

He first came to Hampton in 1754 as a tenant of what was then known as Hampton House (now called Garrick's Villa), acquiring the copyhold later that same year. In 1755 he built Garrick's Temple in the grounds, as a monument to Shakespeare, and had Roubilliac sculpt a statue of his hero to stand in a niche of the Temple – this is now in the King's Library at the British Museum.

Numerous alterations were made to the house by Robert Adam during Garrick's tenure. These were in two distinct phases: 1755-58 and 1772-73. It is thought that the Villa is an amalgamation of some old cottages, although almost no traces are now left of earlier buildings.

The portico and its arched podium are *c*.1756. Much of the 'brickwork' is in fact 'mathematical tiles', thin tiles overlaid on each other to give the appearance of brick. Other alterations of Garrick's time included the building of the Orangery and the construction of a tunnel under the road to connect to his riverside lawn.

He also bought nearby properties when they became available. These included Orme House in

66. *David Garrick as Benedict in Much Ado about Nothing.*

65. *'View of the estate of the late David Garrick Esq. at Hampton with the Temple of Shakespeare.'*

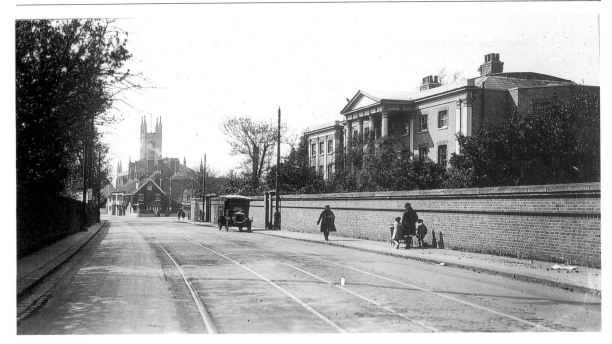

*67. Garrick's villa and St Mary's church at Hampton, c1905.*

*68. Peg Woffington.*

Church Street, the White Hart (then called the Six Bells), and several aits in the river, including what became Garrick's Ait. He bought The Cedars (now known as Garrick's House) for his nephew David. The garden of this property adjoined his own riverside garden – the *Astoria* is now moored beside it.

Garrick collected books and bric-a-brac and after the death of his wife, Eva, at the age of 98 in 1822, the sale of items from the house took ten days.

## PEG WOFFINGTON

Margaret 'Peg' Woffington (1714-60) was Garrick's lover and almost as famous as he on the stage. She came from Ireland in 1740 and took London by storm for her portrayal of Sir Harry Wilder in George Farquhar's comedy *The Constant Couple* at the Theatre Royal, Drury Lane. She also captured the heart of Garrick and before long set up house with him.

However, the long-anticipated marriage did not take place and Peg left him in 1744. While looking for a country house, she heard of Teddington Place, the former home of a Lord Mayor of London, Sir Charles Duncombe. From here she launched her sister Mary (usually called Polly) into the theatrical profession, when she staged a performance of *The Distressed Mother* with the aid of Sheridan and Garrick; Polly was in the lead and Peg and other actors were in supporting roles.

A large barn in the neighbourhood (probably in

Broom Road) was fitted as a temporary theatre and the performance opened to a packed audience. Reports indicate that Polly Woffington was rather wooden in the role and that the show was stolen by the performance of George Anne Bellamy, an unknown actress.

Shortly after this, Polly met Captain Robert Cholmondeley and they were married in 1746.

Peg Woffington continued on the stage and had many well publicised quarrels with actresses Kitty Clive and George Anne Bellamy. In May 1757, when she was playing in *As You Like it* at Covent Garden, she suffered a stroke from which she never fully recovered.

She died in 1760 at Queen Square and is buried at St Mary's Teddington. Her last acts included one of reconciliation with her old rival, Mrs Bellamy.

A row of terraced cottages in the High Street bears her name with a plaque dated 1759, and it is popularly believed that she left these to the poor of the parish. Although there is nothing to substantiate this, the buildings were certainly noted as 'Margaret Woffington Cottages' in an early census.

## JOHN BEARD

Another celebrated actor, who was a contemporary of Garrick, was John Beard (c.1717-91), who lived at the property called Rose Hill (now Hampton library). He was chiefly known as a singer, and his reputation was gained at Covent Garden for his singing of tenor parts specially written for him by Handel.

His first wife was Lady Henrietta Herbert, daughter of Earl Waldegrave, and his second wife, Charlotte, was a daughter of the famous theatre manager, John Rich. Beard retired from the stage in 1767 after he had lost his hearing. He is buried in the vault of Hampton church, and the road Beards Hill commemorates him.

## JOHN WALTER

John Walter (1739-1812), the founder of *The Times*, was born in London, the son of a coal merchant whose business he took over. In 1781 he disposed of the firm to concentrate on his venture as a Lloyd's underwriter, which was suffering from the heavy losses caused by the war in America. However, he was obliged to announce his bankruptcy in 1782, although it was an honourable one with his creditors allowing him time to wind up his affairs to everyone's advantage.

He set up a printing press in 1784 and on 1 January 1785 published the first edition of *The Daily Universal Register*, which consisted of four pages: it sold for 2½d, of which 1½d was Stamp Duty. The name of the paper was changed to *The Times* in 1788, when the circulation was about 1,000, but the change of name

69. *John Walter snr.*

70. *Dorothy Jordan.*

71.  *The Duke of Clarence with the butcher's boy.  Artist unknown.*

did not improve its fortunes.  He lost a libel action brought by the Duke of York in 1789, and was fined £500 and sentenced to two years in Newgate prison. The lawsuit stemmed from an article in which he alleged that the Duke of York would not be happy with the news that his father, George III, had regained his sanity.

In 1795 he handed *The Times* over to his son, William, and retired to Teddington Grove, the house of Moses Franks (designed by Sir William Chambers), and was very soon in court again.

Franks, a Jew, had never claimed his pew at St Mary's, but on moving in to his house Walter claimed it as of right, but the churchwardens declined unless he paid £5 for the privilege.  Walter took the wardens to court, and the case of 'Walter *vs* Gunner and Drury' laid down how far churchwardens had discretion to consider an application for a pew.  On this occasion Walter won his case but was not awarded costs.

Walter plunged into parish life after the death of his wife in 1798, even to the extent of becoming a church-warden himself in 1801.  One of his main achievements was a complete reallocation of pews and the separation of men and women servants in the church.

John Walter died at Teddington and is buried in St Mary's: a plaque has been raised to him on the north wall of the church.

## TWO ROYALS AND A MISTRESS

After a distinguished naval career Prince William became a gentleman of leisure and was created Duke of Clarence and Earl of Munster in 1789.  In 1790 he fell under the spell of an Irish actress, Mrs Dorothy Jordan, whom he pursued relentlessly and finally won over.  She moved into his house in Richmond, Peter-sham Lodge, and began a relationship which was to last twenty years and produce ten children.

On the death of Lady North, William was appointed Ranger to Bushy Park and moved into Bushy House with Mrs Jordan and his large family.  In between producing this FitzClarence brood, Mrs Jordan continued with her stage career, bringing in much needed funds for both of them.  So financially embarrassed was he that in the end the only solution was a wealthy marriage, and despite her years as a devoted mistress and mother, Dorothy Jordan was abandoned in October 1811.  She was playing in the provinces at the time and was completely devastated by the news, to the extent that she broke into tears on stage while playing a comic role.  She eventually died in poor financial straits in Paris in 1816.

William did not find a suitable wife until 1818, when he married Princess Adelaide of Saxe-Meiningen, a delicate young woman 29 years his junior.  From what had begun as an arranged mar-

72. *Queen Adelaide.*

73. *Michael Faraday.*

riage a model relationship developed, with Adelaide taking on the FitzClarences as her own. The couple took an active part in community life and were very popular in the village.

At a dinner party at Windsor Park in 1827, William is reputed to have told the following anecdote:

'I was riding in Bushy Park the other day, on the road between Teddington and Hampton Wick, when I was overtaken by a butcher's boy on horseback, with a tray of meat under his arm.

"Nice pony that of yours, old gentleman!", said he.

"Pretty fair" was my reply.

" Mine's a good 'un too", rejoined he "and I'll trot you to Hampton Wick for a pot o' beer."

I declined the match; and the butcher's boy, as he struck his single spur into the horse's side, exclaimed with a look of contempt, "I thought you were only a muff!"'

William was asleep at Bushy House when he received the news of the death of his brother, George IV, thereby becoming king himself. His ministers arrived at five in the morning to tell him the news. He thanked them and bade them rise from their knees, and after refreshment he begged to be excused to return to bed as he had 'always wished to sleep with a Queen'.

The Clarences are still remembered in Teddington in the pub names, The Clarence, the Queen Adelaide, the Queen Dowager, and in Adelaide Road, Clarence Road and Munster Road.

## MICHAEL FARADAY

Faraday (1791-1867) was one of the greatest physicists. His contribution to scientific advance was acknowledged in his lifetime and he was granted a Grace and Favour residence beside Hampton Court Green in the last years of his life.

## R.D. BLACKMORE

Richard Doddridge Blackmore (1825-1900), author of the novel *Lorna Doone*, was born in Berkshire, though he regarded himself as a Devonian. He was the son of a clergyman, part of a family which had a tradition of supplying ministers for the Church. He became a barrister, specialising in conveyancing, since attacks of epilepsy precluded court work. Despite this, his health deteriorated. He wrote to a friend: 'My medical adviser said I would have to give up my profession, seek an outdoor employment or die young.'

In 1854 he gave up law and with his wife rented a house in Lower Teddington Road, Hampton Wick and became the classics master at Wellesley House School (later Fortescue House), Twickenham. During this period, he was also able to write and published a book of poetry.

Fortunately for Blackmore, his uncle, Henry Knight, rector of Neath, left him a considerable legacy in 1857, and after some thought he 'decided to become a gardener and horticulturist'. To this end he purchased a sixteen-acre plot of land in Teddington and had a house built to his own design, called Gomer House after his favourite dog, a Gordon spaniel.

However, the gardening business was a difficult and unprofitable one. He employed six men on a permanent basis and a further six during the summer months, a fair liability set against the unpredictability of the English weather. He continued with his writing and met with some success with *Clara Vaughan* in 1864 and *Craddock Nowell* in 1866. It was not until 1869 and the publication of *Lorna Doone* that he achieved international fame.

Despite this, his life in Teddington was not entirely satisfactory. His market garden business did not prosper, he had frequent rows with his publisher, his health was far from good and his wife 'scarcely knows what it is to be free from pain.' On top of all this he was engaged in a lengthy legal wrangle with the London & South Western Railway Company. 'If I lose, I may consider myself ruined', he wrote to his brother-in-law; fortunately the judge found against the Company.

Apart from playing chess at the St Alban's Club and attending the parish church, Blackmore does not

74. *Richard Doddridge Blackmore.*

75. *Procession commemorating the centenary in 1925 of the birth of Blackmore. The figure in the top hat is Dr Leeson, Mayor of Twickenham. Behind Mrs Leeson is Richard Blewett, senior reporter of the Richmond & Twickenham Times. The procession is just rounding the bend by Peg Woffington's Cottages.*

seem to have mingled with other Teddington residents. Charles Deayton, the grocer, told an American admirer: 'He has dealt with me for thirty-four years and I have been on speaking terms with him all those years but I have never been inside his garden walls. He is not a social man and seems wedded to his garden in summer and his book writing in winter.'

The plain fact was that Blackmore had little in common with the Teddington middle classes, although there was a definite Gomer House set of other classical writers and most surprisingly, he had a stream of American visitors. He was a strong correspondent with many of these. Although he was a recluse, there is nothing to suggest that he was any less than even tempered and the extent of his good nature is perhaps best illustrated when Gomer the spaniel became paralysed – Blackmore had a special kind of perambulator made to wheel the unfortunate animal about, until it died.

His wife died in 1885 and is buried in Teddington Cemetery. Her nieces, Polly and Eva Pinto-Leite, continued to look after Blackmore, who had become paralysed in his left side. At about this time, he met Violet Veitch, who was later to marry Arthur Coward. Blackmore became godfather to their first son, who unfortunately died of spinal meningitis at the age of seven. He declined, however, to be godfather to their second son, Noel Coward, born in December 1899.

Blackmore died not long afterwards, on 20 January 1900 and was buried in the same grave as his wife at Teddington Cemetery.

## OTHER NOTABLES
Robert Udney (1725-1802) was born in Aberdeenshire and although little is known of his early life, we may assume that he received the education and grooming expected of the Scottish gentry. He became a successful West Indies merchant, made a considerable fortune and married for the second time in 1787 to Margaret or Martha, who was 18 years his junior. They acquired a house in Teddington High Street in 1789, but the following year built another – what became known as Udney House. He felt himself entitled to a 'pugh' in St Mary's, but the churchwardens said that only old parishioners had pews with their houses as of right, and charged him two guineas a year for his.

While travelling abroad he acquired a taste for Italian art and with the aid of his brother John, who was British Consul both at Venice and Leghorn, amasseda collection of international repute. This necessitated the building of a special gallery to house it, although there is some doubt as to whether or not this was within a wing of Udney House or in a separate detached building on the opposite side of the

*76. Robert Udney.*

road. The gallery attracted the attention of George III and Queen Charlotte, who broke their journey to Windsor to breakfast with Udney and inspect the paintings.

Mrs Udney clearly gained an admirer in neighbour Horace Walpole, who wrote 'I have seen Mrs Udney. Oh! she is charming, looks so sensible, and unluckily, so modest'. Mr Udney, he thought, 'looks as old and decrepit as I do.'

Udney House was demolished in 1898.

William Penn, the Quaker and founder of Pennsylvania, issued his denial that he was a papist from Teddington in 1688. Sir Charles Duncombe, Lord Mayor of London in 1709, lived for many years at the house he built, Teddington Place. Francis Manning the poet also lived in the area and wrote about Duncombe's house.

Lord Athlone died at Udney House in 1808 and as there was a fear that his body would be seized because he died in debt, he was buried under the communion table at St Mary's Teddington at 4am. Once his son had repaid all his father's debts he had the remains moved to Ireland and reburied there.

Alexander Herzen, the Russian liberal, spent two years of his exile at Elmfield House (later the headquarters of Teddington Local Board), and was visited there by Garibaldi in 1864.

# A Turnpiked Road

Before the advent of turnpike trusts from the seventeenth century onwards, the care of roads was in the hands of first, the manors, and then the parishes. Though the main highways were 'king's highways' they were still the responsibility of local residents, however much wear and tear was caused by through traffic.

By the Middle Ages goods were being carried in carts with four or more wheels, pulled by four or five horses in single file. As carts became larger and more economical, wider wheels were introduced to stop the carts sinking into the mud and ruts. The larger carts in turn led to more horses to haul them, and even more churning up of the road surface.

The first turnpike trust in the Hampton and Teddington area was established in 1767 for the road from Isleworth to Teddington, and this was followed by another for the Hampton to Staines road. The latter began where the Upper and Lower Sunbury Roads diverge and followed the Upper Sunbury Road, past Kempton Park, over Sunbury Common to Staines, a total distance of 6½ miles. There were 72 trustees, who included John Beard the actor, Lancelot (Capability) Brown, and David Garrick by virtue of ownership of an adjacent estate. The trustees were able to borrow money against the security of potential toll receipts, which could be spent on repairs and maintenance.

Turnpike roads made an enormous difference to the speed of coach traffic. Along their routes inns were part of a highly organised long-distance system of transport that included arrangements for the re-placement and stabling of horses, so that coaches could run to a fixed time-table. Horses were changed at the White Hart, Bell and Red Lion in Hampton and the King's Arms at Hampton Court. There were also short distance coaches to and from London.

The Hampton-Staines turnpike trust was disbanded in 1859, victim of the railway age and the growing competence of local authorities to manage roads.

*78. Part of J. Cary's coaching map for London to Hampton Court, 1799.*

*77. Maps showing the number of stage coaches serving the area daily in 1811 (left) and 1837 (right).*

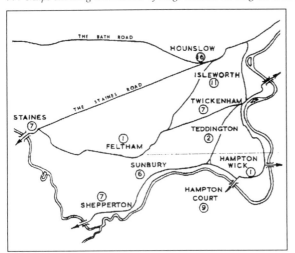

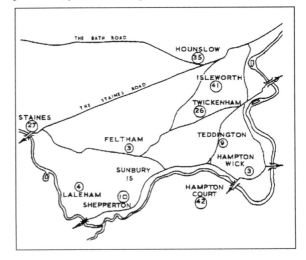

# On Wheels

## THE COMING OF THE RAILWAYS

As elsewhere around London, the coming of railways had a profound effect on the development of both Hampton and Teddington.

The first railway in the area came to Hampton Court in 1849, built by the London & South Western Railway to accommodate the demands of visitors to the Palace once it had been opened to the public in 1838. To comply with the Office of Works requirements, the station was built in keeping with Hampton Court Palace, i.e. of red brick with stone facing, and incorporating gable ends.

The station when built stood on Cigarette Island (named after a houseboat formerly moored there) and was connected to Creek Road, East Molesey via a drawbridge. This arrangement was changed when the present Hampton Court Bridge was built.

Hampton station is on the Shepperton branch of what was the London & South Western Railway. Originally this line, opened in 1864, was to have continued on to Chertsey Bridge, but the part after Shepperton was never built. The line branched off the Twickenham to Kingston main line at what is now

Strawberry Hill station, and four local stations were built: Fulwell, Hampton, Sunbury and Shepperton. At this time it was single track with several passing loops. When Kempton Park racecourse was developed in the 1870s it was made double track and a station opened at the course.

Services were steam operated until the end of 1915, when they were electrified. However, steam-hauled first-class specials still ran to Kempton Park, and there was also a twice-daily steam school train between Twickenham and Hampton. Both these services survived until the outbreak of war in 1939.

The station at Hampton Wick was opened in 1863 on the Twickenham to Kingston line, part of the so-called Kingston loop which enabled trains to leave from London via Richmond on the outward journey and return to London via the line through Teddington and Kingston without the need for turning round.

Teddington was on the main Twickenham to Kingston line, and the station here was opened in 1863. A major upheaval in the parish was caused by the construction of the railway which, among other things, entailed the draining of the village pond and the removal of the local cricket club's pitch to Bushy Park. For over two years the village was divided by the railway works until a road bridge was built over the line.

*79. Hampton Station and old bridge (replaced by the present concrete bridge in the 1930s). The station building on the right dates from the opening of the line in 1864.*

*80. Fulwell station. The name of this station at Hampton Hill is thought to be derived from Full or Foul Well. The name is first mentioned c.1450.*

*81. Teddington station, opened in 1863. This view from the Station Road side.*

*82. Staff at Hampton station in 1910.*

*83. The first electric tramcar to cross a Thames bridge (Kingston) with Hampton Wick in the background (1906).*

## ON THE ROADS

Horse buses were introduced in Hampton from 1829 and by 1840 there were five a day from the Bell to London. Just before the railways came to the area the service to London was even better – one bus every twenty minutes between 9am and 9pm, though this would not of course have catered for commuters into London.

Electric trams came in 1903. There were two routes. One came from Stanley Road via Teddington and Hampton Wick to Hampton Court – this served as an extension to a line from Richmond Bridge to Stanley Road. The other also came from the junction at Stanley Road (where it connected to a track to Shepherds Bush) and went in a loop via Hampton Hill, Hampton and down to Hampton Court.

Around this time many tram routes were being constructed all over west London by London United Tramways, under the energetic chairmanship of Sir Clifton Robinson. Many were the subject of protracted negotiation over compensation. Originally LUT had obtained authorisation for a single track along the then narrow Hampton Court Road between Hampton and the Palace. In the event Robinson managed to negotiate a strip of land from the edge of Hampton Court Green and Bushy Park, and as part of this arrangement the LUT also purchased Garrick Villa, which lost 20 feet of its frontage because of the road widening involved. In the event, Sir Clifton and Lady Robinson lived in Garrick Villa and even had their own tram siding leading into the grounds of the villa from near the corner of Church Street.

To compensate for the loss of land at the edge of Bushy Park, part of the grounds of Garrick Villa were given over to the park. This included Garrick's Mound, an ornamental hillock constructed as a place for David Garrick to view the surrounding countryside and river. This mound was rediscovered in a 1993 survey of Bushy Park by Tom Greeves.

Some buildings went in the road widening to accommodate trams. These included the William IV pub and some cottages at the junction of Hampton Court Road and Church Street. In Hampton Wick all the buildings in High Street on the side away from the river were demolished.

In 1908 buildings were taken down or set back in Hampton Hill High Street when the tramway was converted from single to double track. These included the fire station, then just south of the Star public house, which had been built only ten years earlier.

In the early 1930s the trams were replaced by trolleybuses, which themselves were superseded in thirty years by conventional buses.

84. *Four decorated trams outside Garrick's Villa (home of Sir Clifton Robinson, chairman of London United Tramways), probably for a staff and children treat in the grounds of the villa.*

85.  A 'Diddler' trolleybus outside Fulwell depot

86.  London's last trolleybus, 8 May 1962, at Fulwell depot.

# A Leisurely Life

The amenities of both the riverside and Bushy Park have ensured a good array of local sports and recreations, some simple, some very organised.

There is a nice anecdote about Bushy Park and kite flying told by George Ayliffe, referring to an incident in 1829. As a boy living in Hampton Wick, he was presented with his first kite, which he took to Bushy Park to fly. No sport of any kind was then allowed there to the public and he had not been flying his kite for long before a gentleman came up to him and said that he was not allowed to do it. The gentleman asked him his name, age, where he lived and whether he went to school and, after receiving satisfactory replies, said: "Well, you are a good boy, George; you may fly your kite here whenever you like. If Sawyer [the park ranger] says anything to you, tell him the gentleman who owns the park says you are to fly your kite here."

The gentleman then shook hands and went away and the boy afterwards learnt that he had spoken to the Duke of Clarence, the future William IV. On several occasions afterwards, young Ayliffe met the Duke in the park, and he always stopped and shook hands with the young lad and asked after his welfare.

Bushy Park was declared open to the public in 1838 and it immediately proved to be a great attraction for large numbers of people. Chestnut Sunday was established as a traditional picnic day when crowds would flock to see the blossom on the horse chestnut trees in Chestnut Avenue. This tradition has recently been revived by the Hampton Wick Association.

## CRICKET

Teddington Cricket Club for many years played on a cricket green taken by the railway in the early 1860s. They then moved to Bushy Park in 1863. At the same time Hampton Wick Cricket Club, which was just being formed, was given permission to play in the park as well, and the first match between the two clubs in the Park was on 21 July 1863. Hampton Hill Cricket Club, formed in 1855, also moved into the Park in 1890.

The last club to move to Bushy was Teddington Town, formed originally as St Peter and St Paul's Cricket Club. It was made up of shopkeepers and

*87. Teddington Town Cricket Club c1924.*

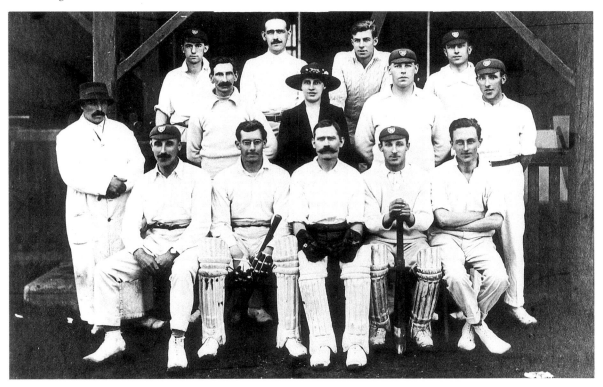

88.  Cricket at Molesey Hurst c.1790.  This painting, which hangs in the Long Room at Lord's, shows a cricket match in progress with a fine and detailed view of Hampton village in the background.

therefore played on a Wednesday (the traditional local half-day) and Sundays.

Molesey Hurst was a very early venue for cricket and ranked with Hambledon in this respect – many of the best teams used to play there. A painting in the Long Room at Lord's shows a match in progress on the Hurst in *c*.1790 and, incidentally, gives a very fine and detailed view of Hampton village along the riverside in the background.

Hampton's first cricket club, The Clarence, was founded under the active patronage of the Duke of Clarence and had its pitch on the Hurst. This club ceased to exist in the 1870s, was revived in 1881, but later dropped the name Clarence and set up its home in Bushy Park.

## THE DISCOVERY OF HOCKEY

The modern game of hockey stems from the activities of the players of the Teddington Cricket Club, who wanted a sport to play in the winter months. A half-hearted attempt was made to introduce Association Football, but instead informal knockabouts using a cricket ball and a variety of sticks were more popular. The poor summer of 1871 in which five inches of rain fell during the last four weeks of the season, gave the players a period in which they formulated a code of

rules for the game of hockey as it is played today. A minute book includes an entry for 10 October 1874 in which those rules were amended.

Sportsmen at Richmond and Surbiton heard of this new game and wanted to form their own clubs. Teddington in 1874 offered practical help by sending some of its players to demonstrate the game and its rules, and the three clubs then started playing each other and match reports began to appear in local newspapers.

This encouraged the formation of more clubs – the Strollers, Upper Tooting, East Surrey and Sutton. These seven clubs then formed the first Hockey Association, which unfortunately floundered. Other types of hockey were being played in Britain, especially in Blackheath and Bristol, and it was too early to impose a standard rule book on other established clubs.

A new attempt was made in 1886, and the second Hockey Association was successful. The knockabout game started by bored Teddington cricketers grew into an international sport.

## FISHING

The stretch of Thames bordering Hampton and Teddington had its angling heyday over 200 years ago. Even earlier than that, the quantities of salmon

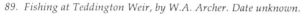

*89. Fishing at Teddington Weir, by W.A. Archer. Date unknown.*

90. *Fishing near Hampton church; published 1809.*

91. *Fishing on the Thames with Hampton church and Garrick's garden temple on the opposite bank.*

92.  *Hurst Park race course in c.1905*

93.  *The scene at Hurst Park course after a fire, begun by suffragettes in 1913, destroyed the grandstand and royal box.*

taken at Hampton Wick and Kingston during the fifteenth and sixteenth centuries were famous.

In the nineteenth century a combination of netting by professional fisherman and the activities of poachers depleted the stocks of fish and caused a group of leading anglers to form the Thames Angling Preservation Society. This was founded at the Bell, Hampton on 17 March 1838. The Society set strict rules as to the size of fish that could be caught and the months in which this could happen. They also secured the abolition of netting between Richmond and Staines, and they pressed for fish-ladders to be installed at weirs, principally to ease the progress of salmon upstream to breed. The first two of these were opened at Teddington and Molesey/Hampton weirs in 1866 by the Thames Conservancy Board.

In the second half of the nineteenth century the quantity of fish was again in decline due to pollution by riverside industry and the vast extraction of water from the Thames. Three water companies had opened works at Hampton in 1855, following an Act of 1852 which forbad the taking of water from the tidal Thames. Pollution continued to be a major problem affecting fish stocks into the twentieth century, and it was not until 1979 that purity levels had improved enough for stocking with young fish in the upstream tributaries of the Thames. Nowadays it is possible to catch roach, dace, bream and even the odd salmon.

## HAMPTON RACES

Race meetings were held on Molesey Hurst, opposite Hampton, in June and September in the nineteenth century. The June meeting was the more important, and was said to more closely resemble a 'thoroughly good old English fair' than a race meeting. They were attended by all types from gypsies to nobility and even royalty. The Prince of Wales attended in 1881 and presented a prize of £100 for one of the races.

Towards the end of the century competition from other race courses, including Kempton Park, reduced attendances and the last of the old-style Hampton races was held in 1887. Two years later the Hurst Park club was founded using the same location, but in 1913 the Royal Box and the greater part of the grandstand were extensively damaged by a fire begun by suffragettes. Racing continued at Hurst Park until the 1960s when the course was sold and developed as a housing estate.

## FISTICUFFS

Molesey Hurst was also the scene of many prize fights, which attracted great crowds with the inevitable drunkenness and rowdiness. At a fight in 1815 it is recorded that 'upwards of 10,000 persons were congregated on the Hurst to witness this encounter'. At another in 1816 there were 'twenty thousand gath-

*94. Another scene of the fire damage at Hurst Park in 1913.*

95. *Journey to a fight at Molesey Hurst, c.1819. The top picture shows the ferries arriving from Hampton on the Molesey side with the crowds around the ring on the riverbank. The second picture depicts the old Red Lion in its heyday. The third picture shows fight-goers passing the Diana Fountain in Bushy Park and the bottom picture contains another view of the journey to the prize fight.*

ered'. A fight that same year continued to round 68 and lasted an hour and twenty-five minutes. One of the contestants had to be removed to the Red Lion in Hampton to be attended by doctors, but he subsequently died and a verdict of manslaughter was recorded. His opponent stood trial and was sentenced to two months imprisonment.

## RUGBY

The Harlequins Rugby Club was once established in Fairfax Road, but its success and international status caused it to outgrow its ground there and in an exchange with the borough council in 1971, the club acquired the Adrian Stoop Memorial Ground in Twickenham; subsequently the Fairfax Road site was given over to housing, a new school and a school rugby pitch.

In 1966, Old Masonians RFC and the non-employees of Decca RFC joined forces to play rugby in Home Park under the name of Antlers Rugby Club; in 1969 they began using the clubhouse of the Teddington Town Cricket Club during the winter months. In 1981 they adopted the town name by becoming Antlers Teddington RFC. Now in their thirtieth season, they continue to flourish and have added a Ladies XV to their complement.

## LAWN TENNIS

Organised tennis in Teddington began with the Baptist Sunday School Library which formed a tennis club in 1908. It was called the Queens Road Tennis Club and comprised three, later four grass courts on land owned by Charles Deayton, rented at £10 per year. In 1914 the Club was forced to seek a new home and it opted for a plot in Vicarage Road owned by the executors of the late Mr Ive, a butcher in the High Street, again at a rent of £10 per annum. Following this move, the club changed its name to Teddington Lawn Tennis Club.

By 1922 the Club was given the option to buy the ground or dissolve. The members decided on the former, and the price of £900 was paid personally by the Club secretary, A.E. Cave. He then leased the ground to the Club and this generous and far-sighted act kept the Club in existence. Hard courts were then introduced as well.

The Club celebrated its silver jubilee in 1958 in great style and in a position of financial strength. It has developed into one of the premier tennis clubs in south London.

96. *Four men in a boat on the river at Hampton; date unknown.*

97. *This turn of the century photograph sums up the attractions of Teddington weir and lock on a sunny day.*

# Installations on the Thames

## THE WATERWORKS

Several waterworks came to Hampton after the first Metropolis Water Act of 1852. The government, at last prodded into action to deal with the vastly polluted water being offered to Londoners, forbad the companies to obtain water from the tidal reaches of the Thames. In effect, this meant any Thames water had to be taken upstream of Teddington lock. As a consequence, by 1855 the Southwark & Vauxhall, the Grand Junction and the West Middlesex Water Companies had all established works at Hampton.

Later, the Metropolis Water Act 1902 placed these companies in the hands of the Metropolitan Water Board (est. 1903), and this remained the situation

until the Thames Water Authority was formed in 1973, since privatised as Thames Water plc.

The waterworks were to change the character of Hampton. Apart from the construction of massive engine houses and ancillary buildings, there were filter beds and reservoirs. Not only did these utilise large tracts of land, but they also prevented access to a substantial area of Hampton riverside, thus significantly reducing the amenities of Hampton.

The pumping stations were among the largest in the world at the time. The daily total capacity of the systems was over 100 million gallons of water, which used over 100 tons of coal. This coal was generally brought up river on barges, although in times of flood, when the coal wharf could not be used, it came by train. In either case the coal was then hauled by horse and cart to the pumping stations, which was not a satisfactory situation because of the poor condition of the roads and the frequent disputes among river workers.

To resolve these unpredictable transport arrangements, a narrow gauge (two foot) railway – the Metropolitan Water Board Light Railway – was constructed in 1915. This connected the coal wharf to the

*98. Plan of the waterworks and reservoirs at Hampton 1901.*

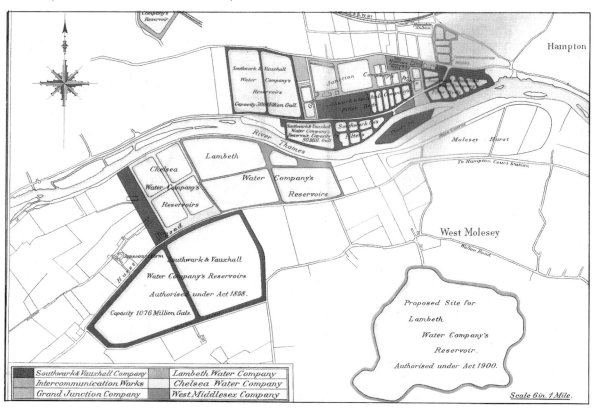

pumping stations in Hampton, as well as the Kempton Park pumping station. In addition it also joined with a standard gauge railway siding at Sunbury station so that coal could be transported from the Shepperton line to the smaller narrow gauge waggons, of which there were around 140.

The narrow track extended to around 3½ miles in total. Apart from its connections to various boiler houses and workshops, it crossed the Lower Sunbury Road, ran under the Upper Sunbury Road and along-side the L&SWR line until it passed under that line and crossed Kempton Park Lane at a level crossing – the remnants of the track and gates may still be seen to this day. From here it proceeded to Kempton pumping station and the siding at Sunbury station.

Three engines were used on this railway named *Hampton*, *Kempton* and *Sunbury*. The line continued in use until around the last war.

99. *(Top) The waterworks at Hampton, c.1906.*

100. *(Top right) Engine of the Metropolitan Water Board Light Railway, 2ft gauge, c.1920.*

101. *(Bottom right) Engine of the Metropolitan Water Board Light Railway, c.1920.*

# Places of Learning

## PAROCHIAL SCHOOLS

There were no schools in Hampton or any of the surrounding parishes at the start of the sixteenth century. This changed with a bequest by Robert Hammond in his will of 1556. He left the income from the lease of the Bell inn in Hampton and some land to endow a 'free scoole' for ever. A small building was erected by the parish in the churchyard and the vicar taught the boys of the village for a remuneration of £3 a year. It was a short-lived venture because it lasted only until the late 1560s when, due to the vicar failing to carry out his duties, the endowment property reverted to Mr Hammond's heirs.

In the early seventeenth century a Royal Commission enquired into endowments that had either been lost or had been diverted from their original purposes. By this time the building and land of the Hammond bequest had been bought by an old Hampton family, the Pigeons. What could have been a long, unseemly wrangle over ownership was resolved with the co-operation of the family. The property was returned and indeed an additional contribution was made by the Pigeons towards refounding the school, which has continued in various guises ever since.

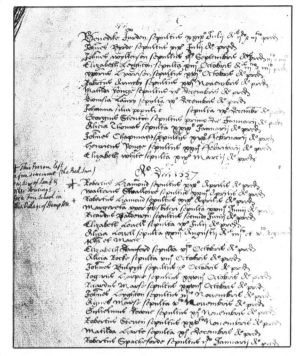

103. *The Hampton burial register of 1557 recording the death of Robert Hammond, founder of Hampton School.*

102. *The former building of the Hampton Grammar School in Upper Sunbury Road. This was built in 1880 to house the Latin (Upper) School which had formerly occupied half of what became the old Parish Hall.*

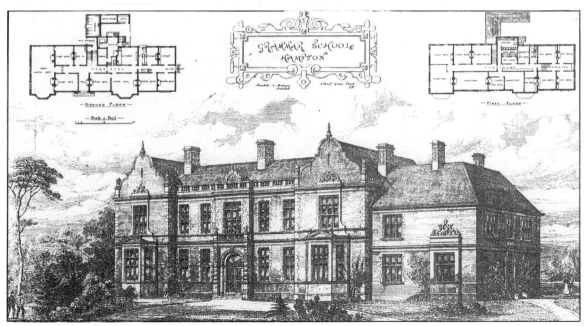

In 1657 a second bequest to benefit the school was made by the Pigeon family. It consisted of stables and land immediately north of the Bell, which was already leased to the inn's landlord, Thomas Ashcombe. The combined endowment was eventually sold by the school in 1933 for over £6,000.

In 1692 Captain John Jones left another large bequest to the school. The income from this was given to the schoolmaster (less £36 to provide pensions for six 'aged and poore' local men). This gift, which at last properly funded the school, was administered by eleven trustees who, in effect, formed a governing body. Five years later the executors of Captain Jones transferred to the trustees an additional property – a half share of Nando's, a famous coffee-house in Fleet Street.

By 1726 there was a large new schoolroom on the north side of the chancel of St Mary's church, a room in which the vestrymen also meet. When the church was demolished in 1829 this left the school homeless, since a new schoolroom was not built for another five years on the site of the present Parish Hall. The new school was divided into two – a Latin (upper) school at the north end and an English (lower) school at the south end. This division was not very successful since

104. (*Above*) *Pupils at Station Road School, Hampton in 1906. The school was built in 1874, paid for by the Rev. Fitzroy John Fitzwygram, first vicar and benefactor of Hampton Hill. After the pupils moved to the newly-built Ripley Road School in 1970 it was demolished. A block of flats, Rushbury Court, was built on the site.*

105. (*Below*) *Teachers at Station Road School in 1903.*

the parents of pupils in the mainly middle-class Latin School did not relish the contact with the poorer boys in the other half.

By the late 1860s the Latin School's fortunes were reviving. After selling some of the land from the Jones bequest, a new building was opened for it in 1880 in the Upper Sunbury Road. The school stayed in these premises until its removal in 1939 to the present site in the Hanworth Road. By that time it was known as Hampton Grammar School – it is now the Hampton School. Part of its Rectory Road site was disposed of. On this land the Rectory Secondary Modern School was built by the county, and on the remainder was built the Lady Eleanor Holles School.

The English School also continued to grow. Its masters included Henry Ripley, who wrote *The History and Topography of Hampton-on-Thames* (1884), the first published history of Hampton. The school overflowed into the Navvies Mission in Station Road until a new building was opened as the Percy Road School in 1907.

The old school was then made into a parish hall, which was replaced by the present building in 1968.

There was no free education for girls until 1803, when the School of Industry was opened in 1805. Subjects taught were reading, writing and needle-work. The building was later condemned as it did not meet the requirements of the 1870 Education Act, and after use as a working men's club it became the drill hall of G company of the 2nd Volunteer Battalion, Middlesex. Latterly it was a motor works and was demolished in the 1960s. An MOT testing station is now on the site.

In the meantime the girls' school had moved to Station Road where it was established along Anglican lines. Here it remained until it joined the boys' school in Percy Road in 1907. A block of flats, Rushbury Court, is now on the site of the older building.

Teddington Public School was opened by subscription in 1832, with Queen Adelaide as a patron. This was for boys only, but it was expanded in 1843 to include girls and infants, and by 1850 it had 170 pupils.

## AN IMMIGRANT SCHOOL

The Lady Eleanor Holles School was established in 1771 in Hackney as a result of a bequest by Lady Holles in 1708. In 1936-7 it moved to Teddington where it occupied initially the premises of a private school called Summerleigh, and then in September 1937 moved to its present site in Hanworth Road.

106. *Percy Road School, Hampton 1907. This school was built to house the boys who had overflowed the English School and who had temporarily been accommodated in the Navvies Mission in Station Road. The girls from Station Road also moved into Percy Road Council School, as it was then known, at the same time. The infants remained behind until Ripley Road Infants School opened in 1970.*

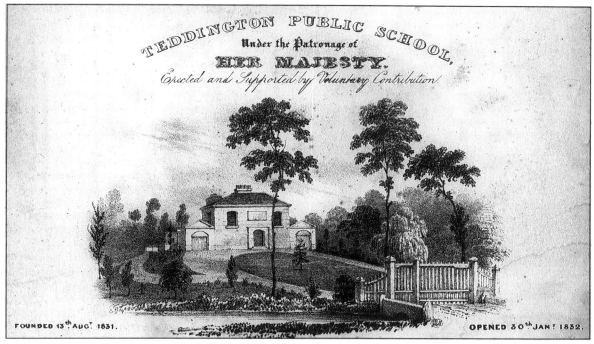

*107. Teddington Public School. This school began with a public appeal on 13 July 1831 which included a generous donation of £100 from Queen Adelaide. It was opened in January 1832, in the High Street by the old pond where SS Peter and Paul Church now stands. It was demolished in 1974 to make way for the new church and moved into a new building in Church Road.*

## PRIVATE ACADEMIES

Many private 'academies' were run in private houses. Some lasted only a few years until their owners either retired or gave up for other reasons, but some were long-running. Mr Jackson's school for boys was in the house now known as (no. 84) The Hollies, High Street, Hampton. This probably began in the 1770s and lasted for around forty years. Orme House was a school for girls (Mrs Ancell's school) from *c.*1770 to 1807. In about 1850 this was reopened as a school and boarders were housed next door at the Old Grange.

Mr Walton had an academy in a house between Church Street and High Street *c.*1830, which lasted forty years. Mr Hammond had a Commercial School in Penns Place, also in Church Street, from 1862 for thirty years. Pembroke House School, a preparatory school for boys, was begun in Broad Lane in 1888; this was closed in 1966 to be replaced by new houses in Broad Lane and Albury Close and its playing fields on the opposite side of the road are now taken by Linden House.

The Old Grange was the longest-running private school in Hampton, from around 1800 until 1910. It was at first known as the school of Miss Berryman, who was later joined by Mrs Francis. Eventually, Mrs Francis, who ran the school until she died in 1863 at the age of 84, was succeeded by her nieces and great-nieces.

108.  *The Hampton Volunteer Fire Brigade pictured outside the Southwark & Vauxhall Water Company engine house at Hampton.  The Brigade in August 1899 took the first prize and silver cup at the Open All England Competition for manual teams.*

# Putting out Fires

The first Teddington fire engine was bought in 1830 with the vestry beadle in charge – it was kept in Park Lane, next to the lock-up. For a long time in Hampton an 'engine keeper' was responsible for putting out local fires. The churchwardens' accounts of 1789 first mention the maintenance of a parish engine, and in 1865 its keeper was a Mr W. Francis – he held the post for many years.

The system and facilities in general and the fire engine in particular in Hampton sometimes led to a less than adequate response to call-outs. In November 1867, at a 'destructive fire' at Rose Villa (now known as Beveree), residence of a Mr C. Leahy, although the Hampton engine was first on the scene it could do nothing for want of water. A messenger then had to be sent to Twickenham to get the mains supply charged. When the supply of water was finally obtained the hose was too short. Fortunately, assistance was given by other local fire engines. In 1870 it was reported that an hour and sixteen minutes were lost at a recent fire while the engine keeper 'was running all over the place' trying to get the water on. Mr Francis said that a new fire engine was needed and people often called the present one a 'water squirt' – he was often, he complained, insulted in that way at fires.

Fortunately there were not a great many fires to test the inadequate equipment. In fact at a vestry meeting in 1872 it was decided that Mr Francis should exercise the engine at least four times a year – which indicates that it had little use otherwise. In 1873 Francis asked for a new hose and at a vestry meeting soon afterwards the engine was reported to be in a fair state of repair, the small pumps good, but ineffective for the needs of the parish, and the hose imperfect as well as small. It was decided to buy a steam fire engine with 280 feet of hose for £550, but it was a decision that was not implemented.

It was only a catastrophe which brought about much change. In June 1876 there was a fatal fire in Windmill Road at Hampton Hill. One week later a meeting was held to form a volunteer fire brigade (for Hampton Hill) and upwards of thirty inhabitants enlisted their services.

In 1885 the chairman of the vestry expressed the hope that someone would take the initiative and form a volunteer brigade for Hampton. Residents came forward at a series of meetings that year and Robert Graham of St Albans (a large riverside house demolished in 1972) consented to act as captain. He was to

109.  *Hampton Volunteer Fire Brigade outside its fire station in Hampton Hill.  The picture is probably c.1899.  The building was demolished c.1908 to allow road widening to accommodate double tram tracks.  The replacement station was built in Windmill Road and is nowadays the Hampton Hill Library.*

110. *Hampton Volunteer Fire Brigade in a drill competition, c.1905.*

111. *Hampton Volunteer Fire Brigade on parade c.1905.*

112. *Hampton Volunteer Fire Brigade in 1906.*

be a considerable influence on the brigade and was associated with it up to his death in 1922. (His daughter, Winifred Graham, was a well-known novelist.)

Despite the presence of Graham's new brigade the Bell hotel was totally destroyed by fire in 1892. There was plenty of water, but not enough hands to pump it, emphasising the need for a steam pump.

The Urban District Council in 1895 acquired premises in Thames Street for a fire station. The Hampton brigade merged with the Hampton Hill brigade and the new station was opened in February 1898 (the building is now a photographer's premises)

A year later another station was opened for the Hampton Hill district, in the High Street but this was demolished in c.1908 to make way for tramway widening, and it moved to Windmill Road, a building which is now the home of Hampton Hill library.

The old manual engine of the Hampton brigade was installed at Hampton Hill, and delivery was taken of a steam fire-engine borrowed from the Southwark & Vauxhall Water Company. Only in 1900, some thirty years after Mr Francis complained about the ineffectiveness of his water squirt, was a steam engine purchased for Hampton.

# Villages into Towns

The two villages had similar problems in dealing with the poor. Teddington was particularly resolute in discouraging outside poor as we have seen (p26) and in 1822 appointed a herdsman who also had the job of 'disturbing all beggars found wandering the village' – he was also known as the 'vagrant driver'. This was clearly not a sought-after parish job and in 1830 it is recorded that 'Robinson's wife be employed to drive vagrants out of the parish, as a punishment for her living in adultery'. Teddington did have some almshouses in Park Lane for the poor, the result of a seventeenth-century bequest by Matthias Perkins and others. The vestry declined to have a workhouse and farmed out the rest of their poor to Hampton, but in 1831 Teddington converted their almshouses into a small workhouse, which closed in 1838 when the parish, for poor relief purposes, became part of the Kingston Union. The old building was demolished in redevelopment in 1955.

Hampton had a poor house from c.1723 to 1770 near the White Hart, known as the Cross House, a former farmhouse. In 1770 a new workhouse was built at the junction of the Hanworth and Uxbridge Roads, costing £400. It contained six bedrooms to house up to forty people (including some from Hampton Wick and Teddington).

Originally the workhouse was supervised by a small committee appointed by the vestry. From 1819 a select vestry of twenty important residents was appointed on an annual basis to oversee the administration. Like Teddington above, Hampton became part of the Kingston Union and the Hampton workhouse was closed and then demolished in 1846.

## THE HAMPTON BOARD

The railways changed the two villages into small towns. With an increase in population and size came a consequent sophistication of local government, but even before the railways the old system was changing. In 1858 power began to slip away from vestries. An Act that year permitted the establishment of elected Local Boards, with powers to borrow money based on long-term potential revenue, rather than function, as the vestry had, on a hand-to-mouth, year by year approach. Local boards from then on could undertake capital projects such as sewage disposal, drainage and street lighting.

To form a Board a simple majority of ratepayers had to vote for it. In 1863 Hampton Wick established one, but in Hampton it was a different story – there, in 1865, the residents voted two to one against such a step. It was to their disadvantage for in 1872 Hamp-

113. *Hampton Local Board (1890-94) drain cover.*

114. *Hampton Urban District council election poster in 1896.*

## VOTE FOR
## FISHER

On the 8th January last year, when he was unanimously elected Chairman,

Mr. DE WETTE said (in declining that office, to which Mr. Larcombe had proposed him) : —

"Mr. Fisher made a most excellent chairman, and it would, he was sure, be more to the advantage of the Council that Mr. Fisher should preside over its future destinies than himself."

Mr. AUSTIN seconded, remarking " that the Council would not be doing right in electing any other member if Mr. Fisher would accept the position, more especially as he had done so well in the past, and they had so many matters in hand just now, above all, the Sewage Scheme."

Mr. LARCOMBE said :—

"As far as his experience had gone, Mr. Fisher was the best man sitting round the table to preside over their deliberations, and he should be extremely pleased if Mr. Fisher could see his way to accept the position, and the further honour of a J.P."

Mr. EMBLETON said :—

"He should regret to see the chair occupied by anyone else than Mr. Fisher, who had the whole of the details of the public business in his hands, and knew its officers from the formation of the Local Board up to the present time. With the Sewage Scheme before them, it was very important to have as chairman a gentleman possessing such practical knowledge of the whole affair as Mr. Fisher."

Mr. GOLDSWORTHY supported the motion (for Mr. FISHER'S Election to the Chair), which was then put, and carried unanimously.

*Present:* Messrs. AUSTIN, GOLDSWORTHY, DENNING, ROSS, MOORES, SANDERS, LARCOMBE, KENT, STOLEY, KEYES, DE WETTE, EMBLETON, FISHER, DRAPER, and Capt. CHRISTIE.

*Extracts vide " Surrey Comet," 12th January, 1895.*

**Having quoted these well-known and experienced gentlemen's statements, I leave it to the sober-minded inhabitants of the District to judge whether Mr. Fisher's non-election to the Council would be a calamity or not at the present time.**

**ARTHUR CHRISTIE.**

115.  *American Buildings in Broad Street, Teddington in 1898. The reason for the celebratory flags is unknown.*

ton had no choice but to be part of the Kingston Rural Sanitary Authority and this subservience, or so it seemed, to Kingston encouraged the residents of Hampton to look again at their own local government system. When a vote on the matter was held in 1884 the residents were in favour of setting up a Board, but permission was not granted as it was considered that Hampton was too small an area.

However, six years later Hampton at last had its Board, and in 1895 it was an Urban District Council. Despite the brief existence of that first Board evidence of its short life remains today on the pavements – a number of drain covers in Hampton carry the words Hampton Local Board.

One of the most urgent tasks of that early Board was indeed the construction of a proper sewage disposal system. This it got on with quickly, although the building of a sewage disposal works at the north-western boundary of the parish did not actually begin until 1896, by which time the Urban District Council had replaced the Board. The first house was connected to the new system in 1898 and by the time the works had been finished they had cost £62,000 which was then equal to the entire rateable value of Hampton! They were, however, considered unique in having the most complete 'biological method' of treating sewage in the country, which involved filtration through various bacteria beds.

Guests at the opening ceremony in October 1899 went by boat to the Island Hotel on Tagg's Island for luncheon, which was served in one of the large, lavishly decorated boathouses.

The District Council functioned until 1937 when Hampton became part of the borough of Twickenham and in 1965 Twickenham itself was merged with Richmond, Teddington and Barnes in the Borough of Richmond upon Thames.

## TEDDINGTON REORGANISED

Teddington residents too declined to establish a local Board, and though two years later they changed their mind their decision was declared illegal; a further local meeting in 1867 managed to take a decision that was accepted by the Home Office.

The new Board was offered accommodation by a Mr William Porter in his house at a rent of £8 per annum and the first meeting approved the seal of the Board – a swan. The rate levied then was 6d in the £1, which brought in about £475.

One of the Board's first undertakings was to acquire land and open a cemetery in Shacklegate Lane in 1879. A recreation ground in Manor Road was acquired in 1881.

As the size of the Board grew it moved into a newly-built Town Hall in the Causeway in 1886 and later acquired Elmfield House on the opposite side of the

*116 and 117.  Two pictures of a traffic-less age, both of the High Street, Hampton Wick.  Above is c.1905 and below is 1902.*

"High Street, Hampton Wick, 1902."

*118. Looking north from Bridge Approach in Teddington, in 1865. In the centre, partly hidden by trees, is Elmfield House, which was taken over by the Teddington Local Board, and to the left is Percy Lodge.*

railway bridge. A fire destroyed the Town Hall in December 1903 and it was never rebuilt.

As with Hampton, an Urban District Council replaced the Board in 1894. This body was responsible for the opening of the suspension bridge (1889), the Carnegie Library (1906) and the swimming baths (1931). After that administration followed the same course as for Hampton above.

## HOUSING

On the break-up of the Udney Park Estate, the UDC put up an estate of houses for rental. Some 124 houses were built in Addison Road – named after the government health minister whose idea it was, Borland Road, after the Rev. Robert Borland, first vicar of St Mark's, and Down Road after Dr. J. Langdon-Down of Normansfield who identified Down's Syndrome. Unfortunately they did not last very long. It was found that they were not suitable for modernisation and they were demolished in 1973-6 and the whole estate completely redeveloped.

Further estates were built in Mays Road (1921) and Shacklegate Lane (1930). The Mays Road houses met a similar fate to those on the Udney Park Estate though Shacklegate Lane fared better.

*119. Down Road was created from the Udney Park Road Estate in 1921. It was built under the government housing policy of the day as part of the national drive to provide houses for rental, and it was regarded as a model estate.*

# Spreading the Word

With both Hampton and Teddington growing rapidly at the end of the nineteenth century the addition of churches became a social necessity. This was especially so in Teddington where the population was rising at a greater rate. The church of St Peter and St Paul in Broad Street was built in 1865 as a chapel-of-ease to the parish church of St Mary, but was made an independent parish in 1880. The original building, by G.E. Street, has since been demolished and a new church erected in 1980. Such was the rate of change that in 1914 the parish of St Peter and St Paul was itself divided to create that of St Michael and St George at Fulwell. The last Anglican church in the area to open was St Mark's in South Teddington in 1939.

## NON-CONFORMISTS

The earliest nonconformists appear in 1810. In Hampton the Independent Chapel was established by Congregationalists in the High Street, Hampton, with a capacity for around 200. It closed in 1868 and the building was converted into two dwellings called Chapel Cottages; later they became a printing works, and in 1980 they were demolished altogether. In 1810 also we have the first record of both a Quaker meeting house and a Wesleyan Methodist chapel in Teddington, but the location of these is unknown.

The Independents also had a chapel in Windmill Road from 1838 to 1870, which is now used by the Spiritualists. They opened a new building in High Street, Hampton Hill in 1870, and this is still in use as the United Reform Church.

The Wesleyans were next to be found in Teddington at Craig Hall in Clarence Road in 1859. This was replaced by a larger chapel in Stanley Road in 1879, a building which was destroyed by a flying bomb in 1944; a Methodist church stands on the site.

In Hampton the first Wesleyan chapel was established in 1861 in Church Street. This was at the initiative of George Urling, grandson of a great friend of John Wesley. Urling used to come to Hampton to fish and longed for a Wesleyan place of worship. He consulted with the governor of Richmond (Wesleyan) Theological College and as a result the students there helped to establish services and then the chapel itself. This church continued until 1925, when the building in Percy Road was opened. The old building is presently used for the repair of electric blankets.

Baptists took over Craig Hall when the Methodists left it in 1879, but they soon outgrew this and moved into a corrugated iron chapel until a permanent church was erected in Church Road in 1895. This was badly damaged by bombing in the last war but it is still functioning as a baptist church.

The baptists were active elsewhere at the same time. They rented a room in Hampton Wick High Street in 1877, moved on to the Assembly Rooms in Park Road, and then built a permanent mission hall in

120. *St Peter and St Paul, Teddington.*

121. *Wesleyan church at the junction of Hampton Road/ Stanley Road, destroyed by a flying bomb on 23 August 1944.*

122. *The church of St John the Baptist, Hampton Wick.*

Upper Teddington Road.

The earliest Roman Catholic activity was in connection with the workers at the linen bleaching grounds in Teddington. By 1882 a chapel was opened in Hampton Wick and two years later, a school was built in Fairfax Road. The ground floor was used as the schoolhouse and the upper floor acted as a chapel until the church of the Sacred Heart was built in 1893. St Theodore's church in Hampton did not open until 1927, although services had been held at various locations by 1897. Early services were at the instigation of Michael Farmer, a cabinet maker who lived in a house called St Winifred's in Belgrade Road. It was in his house that the services were held by his son.

## SHORT-LIVED MISSIONS

The Chalet Mission Hall was a building in the grounds of the Manor House, Hampton from about *c.*1880 until the death of its owner, J.P. Kitchin in 1901. There was also a Milton Road Mission, run by the London City Mission. This brick building opened in 1892 and was in use until the 1920s. Subsequently it was used as a meeting hall by All Saints church until their own hall was built.

A Navvies Mission existed in the 1890s for labourers and others working on the extensions to the Waterworks. It had been briefly placed in Upper Sunbury Road and was later in Station Road in a corrugated iron building.

123. (Top)  Harvest festival at the Methodist church at the junction of Hampton Road and Stanley Road  in 1907.

124.  (Top left)  Hampton Wesleyan chapel (now known as Methodist Church) in Percy Road.

125.  (Bottom left) The corrugated iron Baptist church in Church Road.

126.  (Above)  The first St Theodore's Roman Catholic church in Station Road, Hampton.  This was demolished when the new church was built further back on the same land in 1986.

# The Early Days of Hampton Hill

The area now occupied by Hampton Hill was originally part of Hounslow Heath – a tract of land which covered many thousands of acres and stretched as far as Heathrow. Locally the Hampton Hill area was called The Common and it was still common land at the time of the Enclosure Act of 1811. After this the land was parcelled up and slowly development began, but it needed the impetus of the building of St James' church in 1863 and the coming of the railway in 1864 to transform the area. In 1861 the population of Hampton Hill was approximately 1100, almost doubling to 2100 in 1881 – by 1951 it was 10,500.

Around 1800 the name for the area was New Hampton but the later name of Hampton Hill was sanctioned by the Postmaster General in 1890, though it had been in common use for about twenty years.

There had been isolated buildings before the Enclosure Act. Certainly a windmill was erected around 1785 when John Naylor was granted land on the common to build a smock mill to grind corn and grain. This was demolished in 1876. Its site was on the opposite side of the river from the Windmill pub.

By 1850 there were 24 tradespeople, including three beer houses – the Crown & Anchor (c.1823), the Duke of Wellington (c.1816) and the Duke of Clarence. The rebuilt Crown & Anchor is now Joe's Restaurant.

When the Rev. James Burrow became vicar of Hampton he decided that the Hampton Hill area should have its own church – St James' was consecrated in December 1863. The first vicar, the Rev. Fitzroy John Fitzwygram and his wife were to have a significant effect on the village. They devoted much of their private fortune to building up the infrastructure and amenities of the area. This included getting rid of the hovels which existed in some places and building houses at affordable rents; they also instituted schools, one for girls and infants and another for boys.

When the church was first built it was a simple structure with a nave 67 feet x 24 feet, but there were considerable enlargements in subsequent years, so that by 1887 a tower and spire were added to celebrate the Jubilee of Queen Victoria.

Thus the area of Hampton Hill grew in a few years from obscurity and poverty into a well-formed suburb with good amenities. Any development that followed, and quite a bit did, benefited from the efforts of the Fitzwygrams.

*127. St James' church, Hampton Hill.*

*128. Interior of St James' church.*

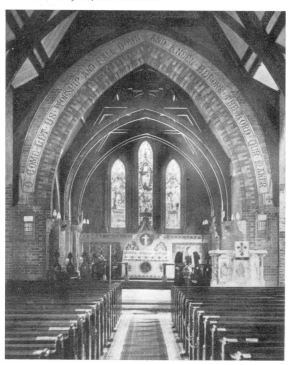

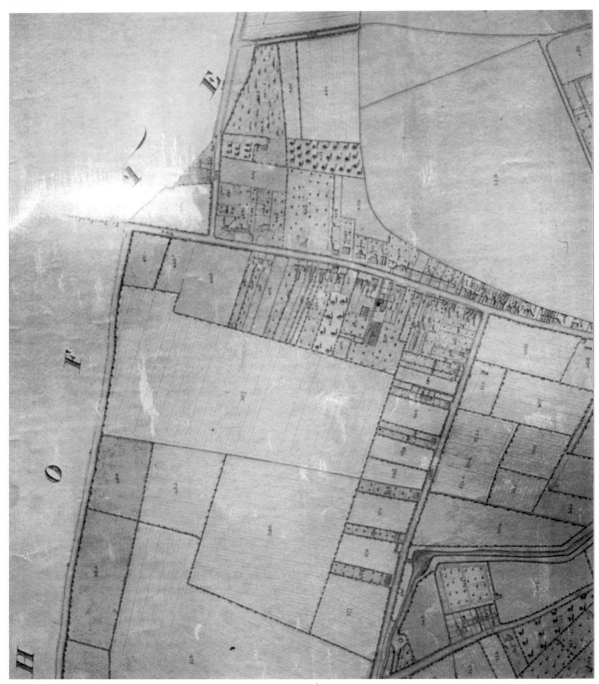

129.  The Hampton Hill area in 1839.  This large scale coloured map covers Hampton and Hampton Hill in sufficient detail for individual dwellings and plots to be recognised.  The road running from left to right is Hampton Hill High Street.  On the left-hand side (from the High Street to the bottom of the page) is Burton's Road – Park Road and St James's Church were not yet built. On the right-hand side (from the High Street to the bottom of the page) is Windmill Road with the Longford river running alongside.  Beside the river near the bottom of the page the circular site of the windmill can just be seen.

# A Tale of Three Pubs

In the seventeenth and eighteenth centuries the most popular inns in Hampton were the Feathers, the Bell and the Shipp (later the Red Lion), all at the heart of the village close to the church. The Feathers still exists, but ceased to be an inn in 1792 and is nowadays divided into three cottages, the middle one of which is called Feathers Cottage. The Bell is still a pub but was rebuilt in 1893 after a fire, and the Red Lion, a 1909 building, has been converted into offices. Their stories are briefly told below:

## THE FEATHERS

The exact date of the Feathers, which still stands on the corner of Thames Street and Church Street is not known. Bernard Garside, the well-known Hampton historian, suggested that it was the building called the 'churchehowse' in the Chantry certificate of 1547. It was probably built *c.*1540 and was not originally a pub at all, but became one early in the seventeenth century. It was parish property for over 400 years until it was sold by the Parochial Trustees in 1973, and the rents from it were used for distribution to parish charities.

The Feathers is a five-bay timber-framed building with a Queen-post roof. The original carpenters' assembly marks (where the timbers were consecu-tively numbered on the ground before assembly) are in Roman numerals and still clearly visible on the roof timbers. Rush-light taper burns can still be seen scorched into one of the trusses upstairs and some old Georgian coins are visible on a downstairs beam where they have been attached with hand-made nails through the middle of the coins.

The first known landlord, Edward Bosworth, had probably taken up occupation in the late 1630s, and there are records of every landlord since. The property was assessed for six hearths in the 1664 Hearth Tax and Bosworth's widow 'Goody' Bosworth paid 2/- towards the new church steeple and bells in 1679 and an additional voluntary gift of another 2/-.

Dr Johnson frequented the Feathers on the occasion of his visits to see David Garrick, but his association with the inn ceased after he borrowed ten guineas from the landlord, which he did not repay. The landlord then went to see Johnson at Hampton House to discuss the matter and in the midst of an altercation Garrick came into the room and paid the money. However, the affair was said to have caused a temporary coolness between the actor and his old tutor.

It is not clear why the Feathers ceased to be an inn *c.*1792. There had certainly been a much greater turnover of landlords in its final years and it may therefore have been the case that an unpopular landlord was the finishing stroke.

The property was then divided into four tenements, with the village blacksmith occupying the rear

130. *The Feathers c.1910.*

131. *The Feathers c.1900. The building on the right is the William IV, which was demolished on 11 March 1903 as the road was to be widened for the coming of the trams.*

yard. The smith closed finally in about 1920 and The Studio (i.e. the modern-day No.1 Church Street) built on its site.

At some stage the four tenements were converted into three cottages. Part of the property was let from 1874 to Henry Ripley, the first historian of Hampton.

## THE BELL

As we have seen (p82) Robert Hammond in 1557 left the income from the lease of the Bell to establish a free school. It was a large building, containing eight hearths in 1674. Samuel Bratherick, who was landlord for over twenty years in the seventeenth century, issued a trade token in 1669 (when there was a shortage of coinage), value one halfpenny, which survives to this day.

Prints and photographs of the old Bell suggest a building that had been considerably altered over the years. In 1819, when the lease was auctioned, one of the conditions of sale was that a large portico, on

pillars, extending some distance into the churchyard, and which formed the entrance to the chief room, be removed and the doorway closed up.

The Bell, unfortunately, was destroyed by fire in 1892; its successor, which still trades, opened the following year on the same site.

## THE SHIPP (RED LION)

It is not known when the Shipp was built. Parts of the old building (burned down in 1908) were certainly very old, possibly Tudor. It is known that by 1661 John Fall was landlord, and that his widow, Elizabeth, provided a meal for Sir Christopher Wren who came to see the new church steeple in 1679.

By 1670 two nearby cottages had been incorporated into the Shipp property and it is believed that 22 Thames Street, which is on their site, may incorporate part of the seventeenth-century structure.

The name was changed to the Red Lion in the late

*132. The Old Bell in c.1870/80.*

1750s and shortly thereafter the Lawrence family became landlords – from 1770 until about 1875. Robert Lawrence was a churchwarden in 1798, a fact recorded on a stone tablet on the southern boundary of the churchyard wall.

The Red Lion was famous for its connection with tulips. Robert Lawrence for many years raised some of the finest new varieties in the country and the elite of tulip fanciers used to attend an annual tulip feast each May at the Red Lion. Later the Metropolitan Society of Florists and amateurs used to hold an annual competition for cut tulips here each May, with the major prize a Ten Guinea Plate donated by Queen Adelaide, patroness of the Society. The garden of the Red Lion was much larger in those days incorporating what became Nos 1-27 Station Road (built *c.*1880 and now replaced by Algar Court) and was enclosed by a 12-foot wall.

In 1880 there was a tragedy on the Thames in which Mr H. Ballard, son of the landlord of the Red Lion, his wife, his two children and two friends were involved. They were all in a gig which was run into and cut down by a steam launch returning from Kingston Regatta, where it had acted as an umpires' launch. The two ladies and children were all drowned, and Mr Ballard and a friend were rescued by the launch.

The present Red Lion was built in 1909 after its predecessor was destroyed by fire (see p24). It closed in 1980, became a restaurant and then was converted into offices.

*133. The present Bell pub in c.1930.*

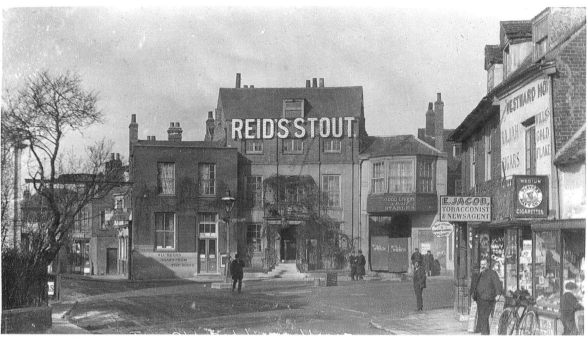

134.  *Near the old Red Lion, Hampton 1908.*

135.  *The old Red Lion, due for redevelopment and rebuilding, was destroyed by fire instead of being demolished, so as to provide fire-fighting practice for the local brigade in 1908.*

*136. The King's Canadian Convalescent Hospital in Bushy Park, in the First World War.*

# Wartime Happenings

### CAMPS IN BUSHY PARK

During the First World War a large camp for Canadian soldiers was constructed in Bushy Park. The grounds and buildings of Upper Lodge were taken for use as a hospital which came to be known as the King's Canadian Hospital. Many of those Canadians who died there are buried in the churchyard of St James' at Hampton Hill.

America entered the Second World War in 1941 after the Japanese attack on Pearl Harbour. One of the bases they set up in this country was in Bushy Park, east of Chestnut Avenue, in 1942. Local legend has it that this was due to a navigational error because the advance party of American soldiers mistook it for Bushey Heath in Hertfordshire. By the time the mistake was discovered, Camp Griffiss was well into construction and it was decided to leave things as they were with the proviso that at the end of hostilities the area of the camp would be returned to parkland.

From June 1942 to December 1943 the camp, festooned with camouflage netting so as not to provide a landmark for enemy bombers, was the HQ of the US Eighth Air Force and from January to October 1944, the HQ to SHAEF, Supreme Headquarters of the Allied Expeditionary Force with Eisenhower its overall commander. From here the invasion of Italy was planned and later the D-Day landings.

In 1994 American and Canadian troops returned to join a Guards Band to commemorate the 50th anniversary of D-Day. A plaque was also unveiled on the site of Eisenhower's old HQ and a newly-planted oak wood was named after him.

In Hampton Wick, by the present cricket club, a smaller base – Unit 12 – was established which became a prisoner-of-war camp for German soldiers. A landing strip was built here and the Chestnut Avenue was also used as a strip for light aircraft.

It is quite remarkable that throughout the war years local residents did not realise the significance of Bushy Park in the efforts of the Allied forces.

Immediately after the war squatters established themselves in some of the huts on Chestnut Avenue. The families were rehoused quickly and the huts destroyed by the Council as it did not want to advertise a surfeit of available housing. Camp Griffiss, the American camp, was finally vacated in October 1962, and despite a battle by the local authority to keep the

137.  Aerial view of Camp Griffiss in April 1947.  Named after Lt. Col. Townsend Griffiss, the first USAAF officer to be killed in Europe, it became the HQ of the 8th US Army Air Force and later of SHAEF, from where Eisenhower planned the D-Day invasion.

amenities for the use of the local community the buildings were bulldozed and the land reverted to parkland.

## DUNKIRK

As part of the preparations for the withdrawal of troops from France at Dunkirk in 1940, all small craft on the Thames were commandeered and used to navigate the wrecks and shallow waters of the Channel to ferry stranded troops to ships lying offshore. The Royal Navy approached all major boatyards on the Medway, Thames and Solent for craft.

Douglas Tough of Tough's Boatyard was co-opted by the Admiralty to marshal all the boats of the Thames and in view of the shortage of experienced seamen with knowledge of the Channel, some of their owners too. He assembled more than 100 ships from the upper Thames to join 600 others in the estuary, where they embarked for the previously little known fishing port of Dunkirk.

Between 26 May and 5 June, under constant enemy fire, they sailed in and out of the shallows taking load after load of soldiers off the beaches. Eventually shelling in daytime became too severe and the operation was restricted to the night. In all, 332,226 English and about 58,000 French soldiers were rescued in this way.

There were losses: about a hundred of the 'little ships' failed to return but such was their durability that there were still a hundred afloat to celebrate the 50th anniversary of the evacuation, with Bob Tough sailing the motor cruiser *Minnehaha*, which his father had found at Ramsgate with her wheelhouse virtually burnt out but with her chart drawer still intact.

## THE BLITZ

The first enemy bomb to fall in this area was on Tudor Avenue, Hampton on 24 August 1940. It caused much damage but no casualties. The intensity of bombing increased and on 7 November two houses in Hampton were hit with five deaths. The worst night was, however, 29 November and is still remembered by some residents. The raid began at 7.20pm and altogether 257 incidents are recorded in the borough's Incident Book for that night. Seventeen people died when the Willoughby pub was hit, the Baltic timber yard and the Baptist church were set alight, more were killed in Railway and Tranmere Roads, and in Shacklegate Lane, fourteen died. Some people from the Walpole Road area were evacuated to the supposed safety of the NPL shelters where unfortunately one of the slit trenches took a direct hit with six fatalities. In all 43 people perished that night and ten more were detained in hospital.

138. *Editing aerial reconnaisance film at the National Physical Laboratory.*

139. *'Little ships' at Dunkirk.*

140. *Bomb damage to shelter trench at the National Physical Laboratory.*

141. *Wesleyan church bombed in Hampton Road. On the morning of 24 August 1944 a flying bomb struck the north side of the church and school hall, damaging the building so badly that it had to be demolished. For the next seven years services were held at No. 8 Hampton Road until the church was rebuilt.*

## THE ADMIRALTY RESEARCH LABORATORY

During the war there was a great deal of activity in Bushy Park at the Admiralty Research Laboratory and the National Physical Laboratory. At the Admiralty, a young scientist named Peter Wright was working on a degaussing system to protect our ships from magnetic mines. This proved so successful that not one naval vessel at Dunkirk was victim of a magnetic mine. In 1942 he developed the system to make midget submarines foil German magnetic detectors on the seabed and in this way our X-Craft midget submarines were able to penetrate the German defences in Norwegian fjords. In 1944 they attacked the German battleship *Tirpitz*, crippling her and effectively putting her out of the war.

Some time after the war, Wright was called up by MI5 and is now universally known as 'Spycatcher'. (Wright died in 1995.)

## BARNES WALLIS

At the National Physical Laboratory another scientist was working on a special bomb to breach the dams of the Ruhr valley, thus depriving the Germans of a good part of their hydro-electric power, so valuable in their steel production.

Barnes Wallis was an aircraft designer for Vickers-Armstrong at Weybridge and he had already been successfully involved with the R100 airship and the Wellesley and Wellington bombers. He nursed the idea of shortening the war by disrupting Germany's steel production by destroying the Ruhr dams, but their massive strength called for a special type of weapon – a 'spherical bomb, a surface torpedo' which was to be dropped onto the water at low level and which would then skim along the surface like a seaside pebble to its target. It would then sink to the base of the dam before exploding.

The technology for the 'bouncing bomb' as it came to be known was developed at the Alfred Yarrow tank

142. *Testing the model of the 'bouncing bomb'.*

of the William Froude Laboratory at the NPL. It was put to devastating effect on 17 May 1943 when 617 Squadron – now the renowned Dambusters - attacked and breached the Mohne and Eder dams and seriously damaged the Sorpe dam.

Another crucial innovation was developed at the National Physical Laboratory. This was the Mulberry floating harbour, used in June 1944 when the Allied forces landed on Normandy beaches which had no natural harbours. The NPL also provided PLUTO, a pipeline across the Channel, which maintained a fuel supply to the invading forces. Two such pipelines were laid from the Isle of Wight to France in August 1944 and these continued to operate at full capacity until the end of the war.

## BRITISH RESTAURANTS

Civilians became familiar with British Restaurants, a peculiarly English solution to provide adequate, nourishing but fairly plain food during the restrictions of wartime. They began in Richmond in 1941. The Mayoress, Mrs Phoebe Leon, was anxious to ensure that nourishing meals were available to the public for a reasonable price. She set up several premises as restaurants and commissioned recipes which would overcome rationing difficulties.

News of the venture reached the Ministry of Food who were much taken with the idea, and Mrs Leon was encouraged to extend the idea to the rest of the nation. Soon, every town had its British Restaurant. In Teddington the premises of the art shop in Broad Street were selected and continued in use until 1946, and in Hampton Wick the old bible warehouse next to the station served the purpose.

143. *Phoebe Leon, founder of the British Restaurants.*

# Making a Living

Farming was the major occupation until the railway came to the area and well after that time there were pockets of agricultural or horticultural activity, such as Anderson's Nurserylands in Teddington which gave employment to itinerant pea-pickers. In 1920 there were still more than 200 people in Teddington employed on the land.

By the nineteenth century the pollution of the Thames had caused the decline of another old local industry – fishing. Eight fishermen are noted in the parish of Teddington in 1845, where the Kemp family was dominant in the business. Here the river was particularly famous for its lamprey and lampern, both eel-like fish which fed off the river bed. These were rarely eaten here but were much sought-after in Holland where they were used as bait for cod and turbot fishing. Cooke's *Topographical and Statistical Description of Middlesex* (1819) notes about forty fish to be found in the Thames including oysters, haddock and whiting. In the latter part of the century fishing became here a leisure pursuit, especially by the weir, rather than a business.

## BOATBUILDING

Though a boatbuilder's called Benn's existed near Benn's Eyot in Hampton in the eighteenth century (see p41), the activity does not seem to have become widely established in the area until about 1850. James Arthur Messenger, having served his apprenticeship on the river, set up for himself in 1848 and by 1861 his yard in Water Lane (later Ferry Road) employed four men and three boys. The business clearly flourished, possibly due to Messenger's reputation as a champion sculler and his appointment as the Queen's Bargemaster in 1862. By 1871 thirty men were employed there and a second yard was opened at Raven's Ait, Kingston. Apart from standard rowing boats and small leisure craft, Messenger gained a reputation for building unusual one-off craft, such as the *Lady Alice*, a five-sectioned boat commissioned by Sir Henry Morton Stanley for his second African expedition, the *Nautilus* canoe for Baden-Powell, and the twin-screw steam launch *Daisy* for the Church Missionary Society for exploration in central Africa.

We have already seen (p41) that Tom Tagg had begun his yard on what became Tagg's Island in 1868. More firms followed. In 1885, R. Simmons and Sons opened the Orleans Boat House near the Anglers Inn, Teddington Lock. However, this does not appear to have been in business after 1910. Robert Porter opened a yard in 1891 and in 1895, as Porter & Brice, took over Messenger's yard. Again, this company does not

*144. Porter & Brice's boatbuilding business on the Thames. This was the old Royal Bargehouse that was afterwards used by James Messenger. Porter & Brice occupied it between 1895 and 1910 and it is now the HQ of the British Motor Yacht Club.*

145.  *The Hampton Hill windmill  (for exact location see map on p.100) was built on what was then the common around 1785.  It was a small mill to grind corn and grain for Hampton residents.  Later it was used to make pearl barley and oatmeal.  It fell into disuse around 1863 and was demolished in 1876.*

146. *Tom Bunn's boatbuilding business at Ferry Road Yard.*

147. *Douglas Tough.*

appear to have survived past 1910.

About 1890 two lightermen/watermen, Alexander Tough and G.J. Henderson joined forces with main moorings at Blackfriars Bridge and a repair yard at Teddington. In 1908 Arthur Tough left the firm to set up a coal business at Teddington wharf but the venture failed. At the same time his son, Douglas, was apprenticed to another small firm run by Tom Bunn at the Ferry Road Yard, which was kept busy supplying vessels for Thornycroft's for the whole of the First World War.

Out of his apprenticeship Douglas, together with his brother Gordon, built a passenger launch *Tigris II* and began carrying passengers between Kingston and Richmond. By 1928 the firm of Tough Brothers was established enough to acquire Bunn's old yard and went fully into repair work, passenger boat service, chandlery and winter storage. They expanded greatly in the Second World War – beginning it with sixteen men and employing 220 at the end. They built over 25 Fairmile craft, midget submarines and several other vessels for the Admiralty.

After the war the yard built many boats for the film industry, which included three state barges for *A Man for All Seasons*, underwater chariots for *The Silent*

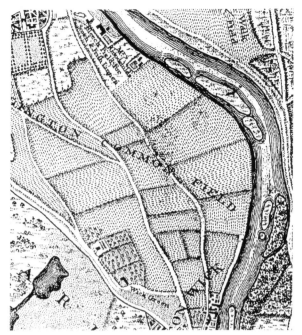

148. *The linen bleach grounds at Teddington shown on John Rocque's map of 1747/8*

149. *The wax candle factory at Teddington*

*Enemy* and a dinghy for *To Russia with Love*.

They also built many conventional vessels such as the *Thame* and *Nore*, both launches for the Port of London Authority, and the *Brave Goose*, a 212-ton yacht, the largest ever built in Teddington.

The depression of the 1980s has caused a decline in boatbuilding and it must be said that the future of the yard is now in doubt. The present head of the firm is Robert Tough, who says that 'Boatyards have never been very profitable – it's more a way of life than profitmaking like other businesses.' We must hope that this activity here by the Thames, now five generations old, will survive.

## LINEN BLEACHING

The earliest recorded industry in the area was noted in John Rocque's map of 1746 which showed 'Mr Goodchild's bleach-field for Scotch and Irish linen'. John Goodchild was a prosperous linen draper and was also elected the first Treasurer of what became the Royal Society of Arts. There is also mention of a factory in the vicinity of these fields between Broom Road and the river. It is not clear if this was connected with Goodchild, but he certainly had premises at Waldegrave Road at some stage. His son succeeded him in 1757 in both the business and in the treasurership, but he was removed from the latter for being in debt two years later.

## CANDLE MAKING

About 1800 Goodchild's factory in Waldegrave Road became the property of Alexander Barclay who established here a wax candle factory. Lewis's *Topographical Dictionary* (1831) recorded that 'It was the largest and most complete establishment.... in the kingdom'. Barclay was living at Elmfield House and his factory became the town's largest employer.

John Pain, a local resident, started work there at the age of ten and later described the process of wax bleaching. The wax was melted by steam and run through a perforated trough over cylinders revolving in cold water, which fashioned it into long shavings. These were taken from the water and spread on tables in the field, exposed to the weather for three weeks and turned each morning. This process was repeated three times after which the wax was white and almost transparent. The company was very successful and it is reputed that the Vatican was numbered amongst its customers. It was acquired by Price's Patent Candle Company and moved to their main works at Battersea.

## PAINT RESEARCH

The departure of the candlemakers was not the end of Goodchild's factory, for in 1926 the Paint Research Association took over the old buildings to establish what became one of the world's major coatings research units. It tests paints and other similar coatings for suitability on a wide variety of surfaces.

## NATIONAL PHYSICAL LABORATORY

This laboratory was established to test and help standardise various machines, and at first was intended to be part of the Royal Observatory at Kew. Under the control of the Royal Society, the embryo organisation began testing scientific instruments and became internationally renowned by the end of the nineteenth century.

The premises at Kew were not suitable and in 1900 the National Physical Laboratory, as it was from then on called, was moved to Bushy House where the upper floor was used as the residence of the Director. It is now the world's foremost measurements and standards office, and its work covers all aspects of physics.

## FILM MAKING

In 1912 a group of music-hall artists led by Bill Killeno scraped together £1,000 and formed Ec-Ko Films. They leased the house and grounds of Weir House in Broom Road and introduced film-making to Teddington. On the grounds they built a huge greenhouse so that they could utilise every hour of daylight for their work – their various activities caused the locals to nickname the place 'Weird House'. In 1928, when talkies were introduced, Weir House was enlarged and the premises were renamed Teddington Film Studios.

*150. The opening of the National Physical Laboratory, by the Prince of Wales, in 1900.*

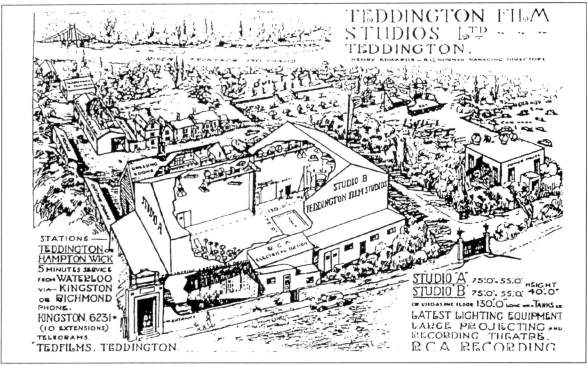

*151. Teddington Film Studios. Under the ownership of Henry Edwards and Edgar Gilbert Norman the studios were put out to hire for independent film makers. This advertisement about 1930 shows a grand entrance which did not exist, a power house on the right hand side which was only in the planning stage and also shows Weir House behind the dressing rooms as being very small whereas it was bigger than the Studios Block.*

The Studios were acquired by Warner Brothers in 1931 for their European production centre. This began a golden period. Feature films starring Bette Davis, James Cagney, Errol Flynn, Douglas Fairbanks jnr, Ida Lupino, Ronald Reagan and many others wre made here. It was estimated then that over 10% of all British films came out of Teddington.

Production was suspended after 5 July 1944 when a flying bomb hit the administration block and blew up the oil tanks. The bomb killed the production manager, 'Doc' Solomon and two other employees. Had it not been for the quick action of men from Tough Brothers spraying their hoses on the concrete vaults, Warner's entire film archive might have been destroyed. Sadly, Solomon declined to go to the Kings Head with the rest of the production crew that night saying, "All you British think about is beer!". The film they were working on, *Flight of Folly*, was completed in a garage in the grounds.

Filming resumed after the war but Warners never attained their pre-war position and in 1955 the studios were sold to ABC Television who used them for

television production; with a change of franchises Thames Television took over in 1968. Despite losing *their* franchise to Carlton TV, Thames are still making programmes at Teddington, but on a much reduced basis.

## MAKING CARS

For a short time there was a car maker in the area. Ward & Avey Ltd set up a factory in Somerset Road, Teddington, and the AV Monocar went into production from 1919 to 1924. It was a single-seater sports car and cost from £146. 5s. 0d for the basic model.

Competition came from the Austin Seven and in the long term this proved too great. AV Motors moved to Park Road in 1924 and continued there as a service station, repair shop and sales showroom until 1984, when the firm closed completely.

Their old factory in Somerset Road was used for the manufacture of metal beer barrels and milk churns, but nowadays is back in use for the car trade and is called The Service Centre.

152. *Filming 'The Murder on the Second Floor' in Teddington High Street, 1929.*

153. *An A.V. Monocar c.1920 with foreman/mechanic Harry Severn at the wheel.*

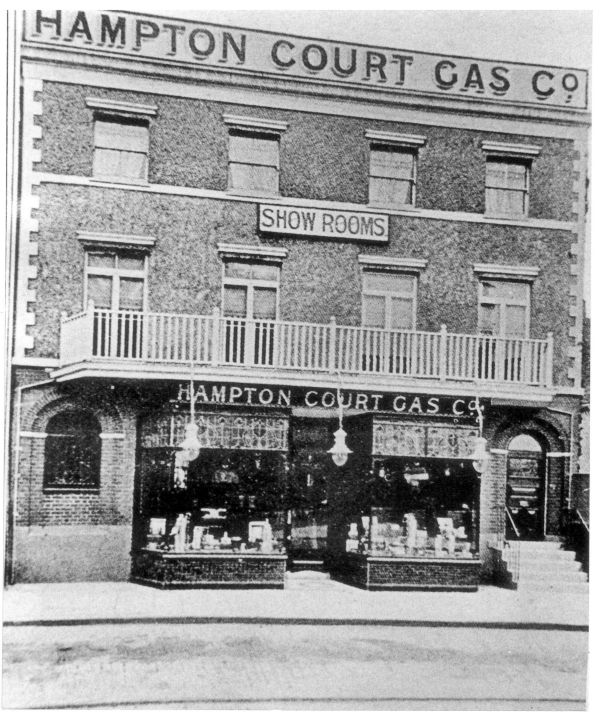

154.  *Hampton Court Gas Company at Bridge Foot, Hampton Wick.  The three gasometers were in Sandy Lane and the last of these was dismantled in 1992.*

# New Estates

Between 1871 and 1901 the population of Hampton grew from 2,600 to 4,200 and Hampton Hill from 1,300 to 2,600. Hampton Wick remained roughly the same, up from 2,200 to 2,600 but Teddington jumped from 4,063 to about 14,000.

Some of the new estates in the area are worth noting. The River Hill estate consisting of Plevna, Varna, Avenue and Belgrade Roads was built along an avenue of trees, formerly in the grounds of Hill House (itself demolished for the construction of the Station Road filter beds in 1902).  The building plots were laid out in 1878, at the time of the Russo-Turkish War, which is believed to be the reason for the road names (there are several Plevna Roads in London), as these towns were in the news at the time.

## THE RAILWAY STATION PRECINCT

When Hampton station opened in 1864 the only approach to it was a private carriage way extending from the southern end of the railway bridge to Percy Road.  Even after double tracks were introduced in 1878 there was no station building on the 'up' (northern) side, and access was gained by crossing the lines or going over a footbridge built in 1894. New station buildings did not appear on the north side until 1897

*156.  Four Hills Cottages in Tudor Road are considerably older than the other properties in the road.  The fact of their being at right-angles to the other houses is one clue to their age.  Their name is derived from the area being known as Four Hills in the seventeenth century and a nearby field was also called Four Hills Close at that time.*

*155  Hampton station with the Jubilee Almshouses to the right.*

*157.   Produce on its way to London from Bartlett's nursery garden, in Hampton. By the turn of the century Hampton had 32 nurseries. In addition to those located on what is now known as Nurserylands, others were in the Ripley Road area. Still more could be found off Broad Lane and around Carlisle Park.*

and Ashley Road was then built.

The railway station precinct of roads dates from about the 1880s until 1905, though there were some older properties there including Four Hills cottages and the houses from those cottages to the corner of Priory Road, and those opposite (Milton Terrace). Oldfield Road, east of Percy Road, was fairly built up by the 1890s, although the Council houses were added in 1903, and the War Memorial Cottages are even later.

Immediately north of the railway bridge a row of six single-storey almshouses stood, built in 1723. They were replaced by the Jubilee Almshouses in 1887, but these were not actually opened until 1895 and were not paid for until 1897. Jubilee House, in which the old are still cared for, stands on their site.

## MANOR PARK ESTATE

This estate includes Tudor, Barlow, Wensleydale and Carlisle Roads. The 9th Earl of Carlisle, who was owner of the original estate, obtained permission in 1897 to develop it for housing. He also bought the land to connect Milton Road with the planned Wensleydale Road, i.e. the modern Station Approach which, of course, provided access to the new north side station.

However, when the Earl sold the 125 lots at auction at the Bell in October 1897, only twelve were taken, and the remainder went gradually over many years afterwards. Barlow Road, incidentally, is named after the Earl's godmother, and Wensleydale Road after one of the godmother's trustees.

## HUMBER AND WOLSEY GARDENS ESTATE

This is an area covered by parts of Priory Road, Percy Road, Hollybush Lane, Chestnut Avenue and Malvern Road. The name Humber is derived from Thomas Humber, the bicycle manufacturer, who lived in Hampton Road, Teddington and developed the land in his retirement.

Priory Road was once called Clay Lane, itself a corruption of the Clea Lane shown on Rocque's map of 1754. Hollybush Lane was once Cemetery Lane; it was named after Hollow Bush Close, an old field name used for land just north of this road and west of Percy Road.

## NEW FIELD AND TANGLEY PARK

The area known as the New Field in the seventeenth century extended westwards from approximately Percy Road to the parish boundary. There were very few houses in the area before this century, although nurseries had developed in the 1890s. Mark Hole Lane (named after Mark Hole Field) to the north was changed to Hatherop Road around the turn of this century, presumably after Hatherop House, a local farmhouse. Ripley Road was named for Henry Ripley, the Hampton historian.

Tangley Park estate, bounded by Broad Lane, Uxbridge Road, Acacia Road, Buckingham Road and Oak Avenue, takes its name from a local farm, whose farmhouse was in Marlborough Road – it was a building of at least 1620, and it was demolished in the 1960s.

The estate was sold in 1865. In 1869 a hotel was built which later became the Female Orphan Home (founded 1855 in Walthamstow), a small portion of which survived as a hall used for church purposes.

A Major W.B. Marling bought the estate and changed its name to Marling Park in 1890, but housing development was still very slow so that much of the nursery land survived until the 1970s.

158.  *The Manor House, Hampton, which stood in modern Manor Gardens, was an eighteenth-century building that had replaced one of the previous century.  The pillars shown have been incorporated into No. 14 Manor Gardens, which stands on the site of the old manor house.*

159.  *The Manor House, Hampton in its final summer, pictured on Jubilee Day in 1935 shortly before its demolition.  The photo was taken by Edward Yates, a local historian, who wrote on Hampton and Hampton Court.*

160. *Wensleydale Road with the shops in Station Approach on the left. Wensleydale Road was named after one of the Trustees of the will of the 9th Earl of Carlisle. The Earl was the owner of the Manor Park estate and the trustee became Baron Wensleydale.*

161. *Priory Road is a very old road. It marks the northern boundary of the large Old Field, Oldfield Road traces the western and southern boundaries, and part of Tudor Road completes the eastern boundary. On Rocque's map of 1754 Priory Road is shown as Clea (later Clay) Lane.*

162.  *The Old Farm House which stood in Marlborough Road, was in existence by 1620.  It was known as Newhouse Farm in earlier times, an isolated building on the edge of Hampton.  In this century the much-altered building was lived in by Jessie Matthews and her husband Sonnie Hale.  It was demolished in the 1960s.*

163.  *Tangley House was located near the Old Farm House.  It took its name from Tangley Park Farm.*

TANGLEY  HOUSE

HAMPTON  ON  THAMES

164. *The old library (centre right of the picture) in Broad Street, Teddington.*

# Modern Teddington

The amenities of modern towns appeared in Teddington once the Urban District Council had been set up. A free library was opened at Nos 1 and 2 Elfin Villas (so named after their architect, Laurence Finn) in Broad Street. The premises were given rent free for the first year by James Edgell, chairman of the Council, and at this stage most of the books were obtained by donation. There was some dispute, therefore, as to whether or not the Council satisfied the terms of the 1895 Public Library Act, and it was necessary to re-register.

By 1902 the library had 509 books and an appeal was launched for more. Plans were also laid to construct a purpose-built library in Waldegrave Road on part of the grounds of Elmfield House, and in 1906, largely due to the efforts of local worthy, John Charles Buckmaster, the Carnegie Library was opened there. It was designed by a Twickenham architect, Henry Cheers, and built at a cost of £4,857, all of which was met by the philanthropist, Andrew Carnegie.

In December 1903 the new Town Hall in the Causeway was burnt to the ground and the Council took refuge in Elmfield House, where it remained. The Town Hall was not rebuilt and neither was the theatre it contained. In fact the only theatre which has emerged in Teddington has been the Teddington Theatre Club, formed in 1927 by a group of local teachers. In 1967 it acquired a permanent home at Hampton Court House and over the years has gained a reputation as one of the foremost societies in the area. With the termination of their lease there, a move is currently being planned to a new purpose-built theatre in Hampton Hill High Street.

There was once a cinema in Teddington. The original building, called the Elmfield, was built in 1900 by Elijah Landen on the site of Percy House. It then showed silent films and at some stage it was rebuilt as the Savoy. By 1937 demand had outstripped the size of this building and another new cinema was built, this time to take over 1,500 people. This closed on 23 April 1960 and was replaced by the AA building which is now Harlequin House.

### THE SUFFRAGETTES

Politics have not loomed large in Teddington history, but there was some suffragette activity in the early part of this century. Some prominent local ladies refused to pay their taxes without representation and on several occasions this resulted in their jewellery being seized and auctioned to meet the tax liability. It was usually purchased by the Women's Tax Resistance League and returned to its former owner.

In April 1913 a train in the sidings at Teddington station was set alight, though the damage was confined to one carriage. There was no doubt that this was the work of suffragettes as their literature was found in other carriages and pinned to a nearby tree. Other carriages were soaked in petrol with candles and cotton wool wads ready for use. The culprits were never discovered but the burnt-out carriage proved to be a tourist attraction for some time.

165,   *The library in Waldegrave Road, designed by Henry Cheers and opened in 1906.*

166.   *The open air swimming pool in Vicarage Road, opened in 1931.*

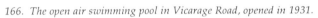

TOWN HALL TEDDINGTON. AFTER THE GREAT FIRE

*167.  The first Teddington Town Hall, after its destruction by fire.*

*168.  Teddington Cemetery in Shacklegate Lane.  Opened in 1879 after the churchyard of St Mary's had been filled to capacity.*

TEDDINGTON CEMETERY

## NEW HOSPITALS

In 1929 the Teddington Memorial Hospital opened in Hampton Road, a culmination of efforts since 1874 when Teddington residents first met to discuss the need for a local hospital. As a result of that meeting the Teddington and Hampton Wick Memorial Hospital opened in February 1875 in Elfin Grove, with one matron and a capacity for up to six patients. A population rise to over 10,000, of course, soon made nonsense of this, even though the capacity was increased to ten beds. This produced a financial crisis which was only solved by a substantial fund-raising effort.

It was decided after the First World War to build a new hospital as a memorial to the war dead. David Anderson offered part of his nurseryland in Hampton Road at an advantageous price, and the energetic chairman of the Hospital Management Committee, F. Hugh Munby, set about raising the money. Arthur Wyatt fully describes the various schemes and events by which this was done in his excellent book *The Story of Teddington's Hospitals*. The foundation stone of the new building was laid by Lord Dawson of Penn on 19 March 1928 and the new hospital opened in November the following year. As Arthur Wyatt noted, 'it was to be Hugh Munby's swan song. A few months later he was dead. He had burnt himself out.'

## THE NEW RECESSION

The recession of the last decade has left its mark on Teddington. The closure of the British Aerospace factory nearby caused the loss of many jobs in the area and the non-renewal of the IBA franchise to Thames Television meant that the workforce at the studios was trimmed to about 25% of its previous size. The NPL and Laboratory of the Government Chemist at Bushy Park have both undergone government pruning with the threat of more to come. The Admiralty Research Laboratory has moved to Portland and the premises at Upper Lodge have just been handed back to the Crown Commissioners. The boatbuilding business is in recession and Tough's yard has not had a major order for some years.

The demise of local shops is very much in evidence as shopping habits have changed in favour of supermarkets. Many old shops have been converted to domestic use, while others have become building society offices, estate agents and antique dealers. Others are still sitting vacant.

There has been a noticeable increase in the volume of traffic through the town. As most of the housing is pre-1935 little or no consideration was given to the incorporation of garages with the houses, with the result that there is a great deal of street parking.

The River Thames and Bushy Park act as two natural boundaries, and there has been little room for expansion. This has meant that many of the older

169. *Teddington Theatre Club c.1946, rehearsing at The Old Hollies in Stanley Road.*

large houses have been pulled down for blocks of smaller houses or flats and some of those that survive have lost their gardens to development. With a building limit of three storeys, nothing new is allowed to upset the balance of the skyline.

However, the desirability of Teddington as a place

to live is as strong as ever with properties holding their values better than in other parts of the country.

One area which has changed has been the High Street which has become the dining centre of the borough, with almost every type of foreign cuisine available.

In 1975 the Haymarket Publishing Group moved into Teddington, taking over Nation House in Hampton Road, the former Head Office of the Nation Life and General Assurance Company, which had been absorbed by one of the insurance giants in the mid 1960s.

170. *The old Savoy cinema, built on the site of The Elmfield cinema; it was demolished in 1937.*

171. *The new Savoy, opened in 1938 with 1574 seats. It was closed in 1962.*

172. *Fund-raising fete for Teddington Hospital, held at The Grove in June 1907.*

The nearby complex of Heathrow Airport provides employment for some of the local population and considerable inconvenience and nuisance to most of them with a world record number of flights going in and out of the airport every day and night. A debate currently rages as to the feasibility and desirability of building a fifth Terminal.

Today, Teddington is almost a dormitory town of London, with hundreds of commuters setting off for their shops and offices via the main line stations of Waterloo and Victoria. A pre-war advertising plaque at Teddington Station, uncovered during redecoration, boasted:

**Southern Rail**
**Waterloo in 32 minutes**

Despite modern technology, the journey now takes 36 minutes, but then that's progress.

173.  *The old hospital in Elfin (so named after the architect Laurence Finn) Grove, opened in 1875.*

174.  *The present hospital, built on the grounds of Anderson's Nursery and opened in 1929.*

# Modern Hampton

As with Teddington, modern amenities began to appear in Hampton only after the formation of the Local Board in 1890, which was superseded by the Urban District Council in 1895. Hampton Wick had formed its own Board in 1863, which also became a UDC in 1895. These new bodies were able to borrow money on the basis of long-term income expectation and attempt projects beyond the financial reach of the old vestries. And so, Hampton saw improvements in sewage disposal (a new works was opened in 1899), drainage, street lighting and roads.

Hampton UDC purchased Rose Hill (the former home of John Beard – see page 57) in 1902 to provide offices (previously the Council had worked from Park House, High Street), and also a Free Library. When Hampton Council amalgamated with Teddington and Twickenham in 1937 to form the Borough of Twickenham these offices were no longer required but the library has remained to this day – after years of neglect its premises were refurbished and extended in 1981.

Unlike Teddington, Hampton never had a Town Hall, although one was proposed in a scheme to celebrate Queen Victoria's Diamond Jubilee in 1897.

The UDC did build an open-air swimming pool. This was constructed in 1914 on part of Bushy Park.

Despite a major refurbishment in 1961, it was closed in an economy drive in 1980. The land it occupied would normally have reverted to the Royal Parks and the pool filled in if it had not been for a last-ditch, long sustained campaign by the local community. Subsequently, this led to the formation of the Hampton Pool Group, which with assistance from the Council, GLC and the Manpower Services Commission, reopened the pool in 1985. This group of volunteers, to whom the Council had transferred the property, renovated the pool complex. Most importantly, they installed water heating which prolonged the season and also vastly increased the numbers using the pool. Admissions in 1993 of 120,000 were ten times those of the unheated Council pool in 1979.

Hampton also had its own Cottage Hospital, newly built in 1912-13 in Upper Sunbury Road. This was founded by an endowment from a wealthy resident, T. Foster-Knowles. The hospital was built on land adjoining the old Grammar School and more land was acquired nearby in 1928, again the gift of Mr Foster-Knowles. It was used as a military hospital in the First World War. During the 1980s and 1990s the work of the hospital was gradually cut back and despite massive community fund-raising efforts, it was closed in 1994.

Other amenities in Hampton included a very small cinema in Station Road, still fondly remembered by many residents and nowadays occupied by Messrs. Aquatint, printers.

*175. The library occupies the ground floor of Rose Hill, which it has done since the UDC purchased the premises in 1902 – at that time the rest of the building was used for council offices. The house was formerly the home of John Beard, the celebrated tenor.*

176. *The open-air swimming pool in High Street, Hampton. This picture is believed to have been taken on the opening day in 1914. Note the primitive diving board!*

177. *The Cottage Hospital in Upper Sunbury Road. The view is at the time of the First World War, when the hospital became a military hospital.*

178.  *The former cinema in Station Road, Hampton, now occupied by Messrs. Aquatint, printers.*

179.  *Thames Street, Hampton looking east c.1905, with both Constable's and Benn's boathouses on the right-hand side and teas offered on both sides of the road.*

180.  *The 'Water Boys' at James Forsyth, market gardeners, Hanworth Road, Hampton, c.1880.  The market gardens were then watered by watering cans, which gives some idea of the employment provided by these enterprises.*

## THE NURSERY LANDS

One of the most significant changes in Hampton this century has been the development of the former nurserylands in the 1970s and 1980s. This land (formerly known as Tangley or Marling Park – see page 121) had long been used for nurseries after the failure to develop it, despite efforts that had started more than a century before.

In 1888 there had been twelve nurseries, 32 by the turn of the century, 45 in 1939, then a decline until there were only eight left in 1973. The Nurserylands development has added approximately 1700 homes and many thousands to the population of Hampton, and with it new housing in Hampton had in essence come to an end, except for any building that might take place on the Waterworks land now owned by Thames Water plc (e.g. Thames Close, completed in 1995, and the proposed Station Road Filter Beds Development Scheme).

## RECENT TIMES

Recent times have not been kind to small shopkeepers all over the country and Hampton is no exception. On the other hand some large businesses have done very well, e.g. the 'new' Sainsbury's on the former St Clare's nursery site in Hampton Hill, which when built was the largest Sainsbury's in the country.

The tendency locally has been for many smaller firms, some of long-established, to retrench or to cease trading altogether. In Hampton, Stacey's the butcher, which had been in the High Street since 1904 (the shop they took had been a butcher's long before that), closed in the 1980s. The pharmacy a few doors down, in business since 1840, did likewise. In Thames Street, Kenton's the Sweet Shop closed in February 1995 after 58 years due to the unrealistic rent that was being asked. This now means that apart from a second-hand bookshop there are no retail shops left on Thames Street. It is hard to imagine that this was once Hampton's premier shopping street but, largely due to the motor car, it is no more. In Hampton Hill the Post Office (run by the Makepeace family for many decades earlier in the century) left the premises in 1995, again the consequence of a rent increase.

It is not all change however: Messrs Kingsbury in Station Road, formerly cycle repairers from around the turn of the century, are still in business, albeit nowadays selling and maintaining cars. Other long-standing local businesses have survived and still provide the reassurance of a friendly name.

Many pubs have been in business for centuries rather than decades. In some cases though the building has been rebuilt the name has been retained.

Despite the many changes there is also much continuity. St Mary's, Hampton, (the present building and its predecessor) have stood on the same site for more than 650 and probably 750 years. This church and its surrounding village heart are a strong reminder of a Hampton of long ago. As we appproach the millennium we should do our best to preserve the past as well as look forward to the future.

*181. Thames Street, Hampton looking west with Wheelers, who ran the Post Office, on the left-hand side, before the Post Office was moved to Station Road. Note the mail cart under the sign for the Crown – a pub which gave up its licence in 1909 and reverted to a private dwelling. The landlords are known back to 1791. The ivy-covered three-storey house in the centre is Jessamine House, demolished in 1956.*

182.  *The premises of Messrs. Kingsbury Motor Cycle Works in 1908 next to the Red Lion on the left of the picture.  Chaplin's the grocer is on the right-hand side with the sun blind pulled down.  Kingsbury's, now selling cars and nearly one hundred years old, are today in Station Road*

# Further Reading

## HAMPTON

Atkins, Frank: *A short guide to the Parish Church of St Mary the Virgin* (1949 and 1977 edns).

Baker, Rowland G.M.: *Thameside Molesey* (1989).

Barnfield, Paul: *Protestant Nonconformity in Twickenham, Whitton, Teddington and the Hamptons* (BOTLHS 59, 1987).

Chaplin, Peter: *The Thames at Hampton* (1967).

Chettle, G.H., Charlton, John and Allan, Juliet: *Hampton Court Palace* (1982, 5th edn.)

Clarke, Brian and Webb, Paul: *Metropolitan Water Board Narrow Gauge Railway at Hampton, Kempton and Sunbury* (1986).

Foster, Peter: *Hospitallers at Hampton in 1338 – pt I: Income and Land Use* (BOTLHS 26, 1973); *pt II: Expenditure* (BOTLHS 30, 1975).

Garside, Bernard: *A Brief History of Hampton School 1557-1957* (1957).

  – *The History of Hampton School from 1556 to 1700* (1931).

  – *The Free School of Robert Hammond in Hampton-on-Thames* (1957).

  – *The Parish Church, Rectory and Vicarage of Hampton-on-Thames during the Sixteenth and Seventeenth Centuries* (1937).

  – *The Lanes and Fields of Hampton Town during the Sixteenth and Seventeenth Centuries* (1953).

  – *Incidents in the History of Hampton-on-Thames during the Sixteenth and Seventeenth Centuries* (1937).

  – *Their Exits and Entrances* (1947).

  – *The Ancient Manor Courts of Hampton-on-Thames during the Seventeenth Century* Parts 1 and 2 (1948 and 1949).

  – *The Manor, Lordships and Great Parks of Hampton Court during the Sixteenth and Seventeenth Centuries* (1951).

  – *Parish Affairs in Hampton Town during the Seventeenth Century* (1954).

Hampton History Group: *The Growth of Hampton and Hampton Hill in the 1890s. Roads and Buildings.* (Typescript 1963).

  – *Hampton in the 1890s – St James' Church, Hampton Hill and the Nonconformist Bodies in Old and New Hampton* (Typescript 1963).

Heath, Gerald: *Hampton in the Nineteenth Century* (BOTLHS 27, 1993, 2nd ed.)

Metropolitan Water Board: *Metropolitan Water Board Fifty Year Review 1903-1953* (1953).

Mitchell, Vic and Smith, Keith: *Branch Lines around Effingham Junction* (1990).

Neaves, Ronald: *From Stagecoach to Trolleybus. A Local History of Transport* (BOTLHS 6, 1966).

Orton, Margery (ed.): *The Birth and Growth of Hampton Hill* (1965).

*Railway World* (magazine) Feb. 1964.

Read, Nicholas: *Sisley and the Thames* (1991).

Richmond upon Thames, London Borough of: *Garrick's Villa and Temple to Shakespeare* (1979).

Ripley, Henry: *The History and Topography of Hampton-on-Thames* (1891, 3rd edn.)

St Theodore's Parish Council: *St Theodore's, Hampton* (1987).

Sheaf, John: *Hampton in the 1890s Through the Eyes of Captain Christie* (BOTLHS 71, 1995).

  – *A Short History of the Feathers, Hampton* (Typescript 1992).

Smeeton, Cyril: *The London United Tramways Vol. 1 – Origins to 1912* (1994).

Smith, Helen R.: *David Garrick 1717-1779* (1979).

*Surrey Comet*: Extracts compiled by Gerald Heath (typescript of items 1854 onwards)

Thames Water Authority: *Thames Water – A Description of the Undertaking* (1980).

Thurley, Simon: *Hampton Court Palace Souvenir Guide Book* (1992, 2nd. edn.).

  – *Henry VIII's Kitchen at Hampton Court* (1990).

*The Times*: Extracts compiled by Gerald Heath (typescript).

Urwin, Alan: *The Hampton Staines Turnpike 1773-1859* (BOTLHS 11, 1968).

  – *The Thames – Hampton to Twickenham: Hazards and Improvements* (BOTLHS 31, 1975).

  – *Hampton and Teddington in 1086 – an analysis of the entry in the Domesday Book* (BOTLHS 2, 1965).

Williams, James: *The History of Tagg's Island* (n.d.).

Wilson, Geoffrey: *London United Tramways 1894-1937* (1971).

Yates, Edward: *Hampton Court* (1935).

*BOTLHS = Borough of Twickenham Local History Society*

# TEDDINGTON

Anstead, C.M.: *Bushy Park – The Hanoverian Rangers* (BOTLHS 17, 1970).

Anstead, C.M. and Heath G.D.: *Bushy Park – Victorian Playground of the People* (BOTLHS 4, 1965).

Barnfield, Paul: *Hampton Wick Baptist Church – Our First Hundred Years* (1980).

Bennett, Herbert E.: *A History of Teddington Methodist Church* (1939).

Blewitt, Richard: *The Udneys of Udney Hall* (Swan and Stag Magazine 1933).

Bowerman, Les: *Kingston Cycling Past and Present* (1989).

Burrell, Arthur: *Early Teddington* (notes).

Chaplin, Peter H.: *The Thames from Source to Tideway* (1988).

Ching, Pamela: *Udney House* (unpublished typescript 1984).

  – *Teddington's most famous minister – Dr Stephen Hales* (Teddington Society Newsletter 1993).

  – *Teddington in 1800 – The Year of the Enclosure* (BOTLHS 51, 1983).

  – *The History of the Roads of Teddington* (unpublished typescript 1989).

Churchill, Graham: *A Modest History of Antlers R.F.C.* (Club handbook 1976).

Dunbar, Janet: *Peg Woffington and her World* (1968).

Dunn, Waldo Hilary: *R.D. Blackmore: a biography* (1956).

English Place Names Society: *The Place Names of Middlesex* (Vol. XVIII).

Foster, Peter and Pyatt, Edward: *Bushy House* (National Physical Laboratory, 1976).

Greeves, Tom: *Bushy Park Middlesex – an Archaeological Survey* (typescript, 1993).

Goddard, E.C.: *A Short History of Teddington and Hampton Police* (typescript, 1976).

Hadow, H.J.: *The Origins of the Laboratory* (NPL, 1969).

  – *Bushy Park and Bushy House* (NPL, 1970).

Harper, Mary: *British Restaurants* (lecture notes)

Harvey, Barbara: *Westminster Abbey and its Estates in the Middle Ages* (1977).

Higson, John: *Lensbury Club* (1990).

Heath, G.D.: *The Formation of the Local Boards of Twickenham, Teddington, Hampton and Hampton Wick* (BOTLHS 10, 1967).

Heath, G.D. and Heath, Joan: *The Women's Suffrage Movement in and around Richmond and Twickenham* (BOTLHS 13, 1968).

Howe, Ken: *Teddington Past and Present* (1994).

Howells, M.K.: *A Century of Modern Hockey 1871-1971* (1971).

*Hughes, D.W.: Tough's of Teddington (typescript, 1978).*

Ingram, Kenneth: *A Short Account of the Parish Church of St Alban the Martyr, Teddington.*

  – *A Short History of the Parish of Teddington* (1906).

Johnson, C.S.: *Totyngton – Teddington* (lecture notes, 1937).

Lysons, Rev. Daniel: *The Environs of London* Vol. III *Middlesex* (1795).

Medway, A.G.: *Teddington Lawn Tennis Club Jubilee 1908-1958* (Club, 1958).

Niven, W.: *Robert Udney's Villa at Teddington* (Home Counties Magazine 1899).

Pain, John: *Wax Candle Factory (Swan and Stag Magazine Vol 1, No 7, 1929).*

Paint Research Association: *Sixty Years of Progress 1926-1986* (PRA, 1986).

Pearce, B.L.: *Free for All – The Public Library Movement in Twickenham* (BOTLHS 55, 1985).

Pyatt, Edward: *A History of the National Physical Laboratory* (1983).

Robinson, G.I. and Hadow H.J.: *The Development of the National Physical Labooratory Site at Teddington 1900-1970* (NPL, 1970).

Royal Parks: *Bushy Park* (1993).

*S.S. Peter and Paul Guide*

*St Mark's Teddington Guide*

Sheaf, John: *The Great Storm in Bushy Park* (BOTLHS Newsletter 1987).

*Teddington Town Cricket Club 1891-1991* (Centenary season brochure 1991).

Tough, Helen: *Boatbuilders on the Thames 1850-1950* (typescript 1981).

Trinder, Rev. Daniel: Historical Notes in the *Teddington Parish Magazine* 1875.

Urwin, Alan: *Population and Housing in 1664 (The Hearth Tax Return)* (BOTLHS 8, 1967).

  – *Twickenham before 704AD* (BOTLHS 45, 1980).

  – *Saxon Twickenham* (BOTLHS 48, 1981).

*Victoria County History of Middlesex* Vols 1, II and III.

Webber, Ronald and Ching, Pamela: *R.D. Blackmore of Teddington* (BOTLHS 44, 1980).

Woodward, E.G.: *Teddington Town and All About it up to 1956* (privately published 1956).

Wyatt, L. Arthur: *The Story of Teddington's Hospitals* (League of Friends of Teddington Hospital, 1986).

# INDEX

### Asterisks denote illustrations